THINKERS

PLUS

A Sampler of Great Philosophers

GERALD F. KREYCHE

UNIVERSITY PRESS OF AMERICA", INC.

LANHAM NEW YORK LONDON

Library of Congress Cataloging in Publication Data

Kreyche, Gerald F.
Thirteen thinkers—plus.

Rev. ed. of: Thirteen thinkers. c1976.
Includes bibliographies.
1. Philosophy—Introductions. 2. Philosophers.
I. Thirteen thinkers. II. Title. III. Title:
13 thinkers—plus.
BD21.K74 1984   190   84-3692
ISBN 0-8191-3888-6 (alk. paper)
ISBN 0-8191-3889-4 (pbk.: alk. paper)

All University Press of America books are produced on acid-free
paper which exceeds the minimum standards set by the National
Historical Publications and Records Commission.

CONTENTS

To Ellie
Friend, Wife, Life Companion

PREFACE TO THE REVISED EDITION

Some years ago, the book *Thirteen Thinkers* came into being. It developed out of a series of radio lectures given over a Chicago FM station. The book met with considerable success, being adopted by a fairly wide variety of colleges and it made the "Best Sellers" list of the University Press of America. Its main use has been to serve as a text for an *Introduction to Philosophy* course. Additionally it has supplemented other texts in various courses in Philosophy as well as in the Humanities. Happily, some have purchased the book on their own, simply to have a general understanding of a sampling of the world's great thinkers.

Based upon my own use of *Thirteen Thinkers*, as well as the suggestions of others who employed it in their classes, and at the urging of the University Press of America, I embarked on revising the work. The revision does not take away from any materials now present, but adds new subject matter and elaborates further both old and new philosophical ideas. Thus, it remains true to its original intent, namely, to present philosophy in as simple yet as accurate a manner as possible.

Too long has philosophy been sullied with the adjective, "esoteric," when in fact there is nothing particularly arcane about it. Philosophy is preeminently practical and worldly and has immediate application for everyday life. The revision notes this even more emphatically than before.

The essential new points of this edition are several. It incorporates an interesting series of *Exercises in Thinking and Reflection*, drawing upon various pithy quotes, *bon mots* and insights of great thinkers. The purpose of presenting these is to get the reader involved in such reflection and to make his own reasoned judgment with respect to their worth and meaning. Additionally, each of the original thirteen thinkers is given much more extensive elaboration and a copious use of examples assures a better understanding of their thought. Some elements of possible critique also work their way into the text, more by way of suggestion, however, rather than as an intrusion upon the exposition of the thinker.

To this work has been added the outlook of two more philosophers, namely, the perennially interesting Socrates, and a man whose thought is being restudied in light of new discoveries about him and his writings, Friedrich Nietzsche. Although both are universally accorded the status of philosophers, no two persons could be philosophically further apart. Yet both speak to our age, an age of moral questioning, an age of social turmoil, an age of intense concern and perhaps even fright. Whatever our age needs it needs courage, and both of these philosophers explicitly demonstrate that virtue in their own personal lives and their own philosophies.

Lastly, I have taken the privilege of appending a *Concluding Essay,* which quite frankly is both expository of my own ideas and exhortatory for the reader.

The title of the book has been altered to *Thirteen Thinkers—Plus,* to indicate the additional entries. It is an appropriate title for several reasons. One is that it rightly suggests continuity with the previous first edition. The second reason is that in English, "plus" signifies primarily what is more and *there is more* in this new edition. But in French, "plus" also implies something special, something that approaches the best. That is how I hope you will view this new edition—as something special. Take it then and, Enjoy! Enjoy!

PREFACE

Most of us, while knowledgeable enough in our own discipline, are basically unacquainted with the fundamental views of famous thinkers in other areas. Worse, we may even be totally ignorant of the nature of the discipline itself or of this or that important figure whose name is common currency for others and whose influence is legend. For example, those who are not professional psychologists, would be hard pressed to sum up the basic ideas of Freud or Jung, yet, these men of genius have had a tremendous impact on how we understand ourselves, our cultures and our times. The same might be said of the non-scientist's understanding of a Newton or Einstein; of the layman's grasp of Dante, Compte, Goethe or Tillich. The list is virtually endless. All of us would like to have at least a familiarity with their views but we have neither the inclination nor time to go through the technical writings by and about the persons themselves.

This book about some philosophers is an attempt to remedy the situation described above, at least with respect to philosophy. It is written so that the reader, presumably one who has not been introduced to the formal study of philosophy, can get a "feel" for what philosophy is about. This is accomplished in part by getting to know philosophers as people, living at various moments in history. When one understands the problems they raise in the perspectives of their lives and writings, one sees more concretely the otherwise abstract nature of philosophy. To emphasize this concrete side of philosophy, the language used throughout is largely nontechnical and ordinary. Where a technical term is employed, it is carefully explained.

The thrust of the book, then, is toward getting across to the general reader, an overview of a number of philosophers and their respective philosophies. The selection of those in the book was based on two principles: first, their overviews should stress questions of value and meaning; second, they should represent the various recognized epochs of the history of Western philosophy.

This book, then, is not meant to be a history of philosophy, but only a "sampler" for the uninitiated. Nonetheless, the selections do represent a flow of ideas from ancient Greece to twentieth century Paris.

One further note must be added. The demands for brevity, coupled with the selective criteria mentioned above, explains why not only many important philosophers but important movements in philosophy have been omitted. The reader interested in these missing movements and men should consult a standard history of philosophy where greater coverage in depth and breadth will be found.

INTRODUCTION

Before we take a look at representative philosophers through the ages, it would be helpful to learn something general about the nature of philosophy itself, how it got started, the directions it took and is taking today.

One might say with Aristotle that philosophy begins as a result of man's tendency to wonder—about things, himself, the world, and God. Clearly, one would not have time for such an intellectual luxury as wonder, until civilization reached a measure of self-sufficiency thereby enabling man to put down his hunting weapons or his farming tools and think. Thus it was that philosophy begins in its more formal sense in the Western world with a man called Thales (624–546 B.C.). He came from the Greek colony, Ionia, now part of Turkey. He was one of the earliest men to break free of magic, myth and religion in his thinking about the nature of things. He sought by means of reason and experience alone, the causes of the world. At this early period, the nature of the cosmos was the chief concern for reflection.

In the ensuing centuries that bring us to Socrates (470–399 B.C.), Plato's mentor, we find philosophy becoming more sophisticated. It spreads out its enquiry to ask about the norms of ethical conduct, the social-political world of man, the nature of motion, of being, of God. In short, around this time, philosophy began "putting it all together" and takes on the general meaning we understand it by today. That meaning of philosophy is as a kind of overview, a philosophy of life, a seeking of the kind of wisdom (to be distinguished from only a technical knowledge of a particular discipline). In this broad sense, philosophy is inescapable for man. Every man is a philosopher of sorts, at least implicitly, for he has overviews, he assesses the relative values of this or that action and, in general, he wonders what life is about. All of these are attempts to apply philosophy, to think philosophically.

Let us elaborate on man being unable to escape philosophy. When looking at a work of art we often question whether it is merely technically proficient or really beautiful. To judge its beauty we must have an implicit standard and understanding of what beauty is, a problem for philosophy of art or aesthetics.

In reading various stories, novels or great books, we find there invariably recurring themes, mostly of a philosophical nature. For example, the theme of good and evil in Melville's *Moby Dick* (exemplified by the Great White Whale and Captain Ahab); the search for life's meaning in Joseph Conrad's *Lord Jim*, *The Secret Sharers* or *Heart of Darkness*; the nature of law and relationship of the individual to it in Victor Hugo's *Les Miserables*; the search for God in any of Graham Green's novels such as *The Power and the Glory*. All these themes are problems for the philosophy of literature.

When we read the *Old Testament* or Toynbee's *Study of History*, we raise or uncover perspectives on the nature of human achievement asking whether there are patterns of progression toward an ultimate goal, retrogression toward an earlier beginning, or perhaps only circularity arguing to the myth of eternal return. These all constitute philosophies of history and may be found in Christianity, e.g., St. Augustine's *City of God* or in Communism, e.g., Plekhanov's *The Role of the Individual in History*.

When we ask about the truth of the methods of modern science, whether its models and constructs mirror or manipulate reality, whether science's laws are discovered in reality or superimposed upon it, we are in the area of philosophy of science.

In a more traditional sense, then, philosophy is all embracing—a specialty of the general. Still since its early days it has undergone considerable evolution. All the way through the Middle Ages, the scientist and the philosopher were the same; in the Middle Ages of the Latin West, the theologian and philosophers were often the same. In the modern era, however, philosophy broke away from theology and science in turn went its way separated from philosophy. Increasingly, the specialized sciences developed, both hard, e.g., physics, and soft, e.g., psychology and sociology.

For some, philosophy remains only a skeleton of its former self, an empty shell. All it can do is be a parasite or critique of other disciplines. It cannot supply new knowledge, but it can keep honest those disciplines that do, by plying its Socratic questions. In a simplified way, this is partly the role of philosophy currently envisaged by the contemporary movement known as Anglo-Saxon philosophy or *linguistic analysis*.

On the other hand, there is an appeal to the dynamic in the equally contemporary philosophical movements of *existentialism* and *process philosophy*. The latter, although associated with the mathematician-philosopher Alfred North Whitehead, bears at least an affinity with the ideas of Henri Bergson and Teilhard de Chardin.

A third strong movement that may be found today is that of *phenomenology*, a method and sometimes a philosophy as well. It is primarily descriptive and concerned with the structure of consciousness. Its popularity is largely continental, however.

Add to the movements mentioned above, that of dialectical philosophy such as Marxism and the residue of *classical* and *intellectualistic* philosophy, such as scholasticism and a sketch has been drawn of the various directions of philosophy today.

Despite the great diversity of philosophical tangents, there nonetheless remain problems and questions perennially valid, stemming from human nature itself and the condition of man in the world. There is no better beginning for a discussion of some of these problems than to start with the thinkers of the "Golden Age" of Greece, Socrates, Plato and Aristotle.

GETTING THE MOST OUT OF THE READINGS

Since the reader presumably is a newcomer to philosophy, the following suggestions are offered as a means of getting the most out of what is read.

1. Read with an explicit purpose, whether it be only that of "browsing" through an individual section or seeking to compare the differences in outlooks between two different philosophers.

2. When finished with one section, demand of yourself a quick review of what you have read. Summarize in your own words the highlights of the reading. This will test your comprehension and continuity of thought and whether your reading has accomplished the goal set beforehand.

3. In your summation, organize what you consider the important points first, then lesser details. Do not ignore details, however. At least know them in a general way. E.g., if you cannot remember the dates of Socrates, Plato and Aristotle, at least mark them as pre-Christian thinkers with Socrates teaching Plato, and Plato being the teacher of Aristotle. Or again, try to recall the dates of Kierkegaard and Marx, but short of that, remember that both were nineteenth century thinkers.

4. To check on your general grasp of the material, try to answer the Self-Tester Review Questions at the end of each reading. These are arranged to follow the progression of the text.

5. To encourage you to reflect for yourself, now try to respond to the Special Thought Question at the end of each section. This is a question for your own judgement; it is not necessarily a question that has a "right" or "wrong" answer. In responding to it, do not afford yourself the luxury of failing to give reasons for your

viewpoint, for it is precisely in the latter that philosophy largely consists.

6. After reading a thinker, ask yourself what he has said that might be pertinent to your own life.

7. When you find a philosopher that you particularly enjoy, consult the bibliography for further reading. Choose either or both the secondary or primary source given. These are selected to promote further easy understanding of the philosopher. E.g., to retain interest in Plato, read the *Apology* rather than the difficult and technical *Parmenides*.

8. At the end of the text is a section entitled, "Exercises in Thinking and Reflecting." These are philosophical statements of various sorts which are meant to be philosophically provocative. Try to deal with one each day by thinking about what it says to you and whether or not you agree with it. Preferably, put your thoughts in writing. There is no substitute for writing to detect sloppiness or clarity of thought.

9. Discuss your ideas about philosophy with others and try to present the main views of a given philosopher as honestly as you can. The criterion for objectivity can be determined by a simple test. Ask yourself if were that philosopher present, could he say, "Yes, that's about what I have held in my philosophy, give or take an exception here or there." If this criterion be met, you can pride yourself on being an honest and serious and understanding student of philosophy.

10. The Glossary of "Isms" provides a handy reference to representative philosophical positions. Try to define them yourself and check your general understanding of them with the descriptions given.

Now let me welcome you to the world of philosophy, a world in which you always have lived, but perhaps never knew it.

Gerald F. Kreyche
DePaul University
Chicago

1
SOCRATES (470–399 B.C.)

"The unexamined life is not worth living."

The Gadfly

Probably the best way to introduce one to Philosophy is to begin with a philosopher who never wrote a word. Such a one is truly an *avis rara*—a rare bird. His name was Socrates and he lived from 470 to 399 B.C. We know of him primarily through his illustrious pupil, Plato. Indeed, he often serves as the chief figure in Plato's *Dialogues*. Whether the character of Socrates as portrayed there is historically accurate is a matter of disputed scholarship, however. Highly revered by Plato, he invariably is the "good guy" of the Dialogues, yet quite clearly as Plato's writings mature, his own ideas take over and Socrates is reduced to the role of a mouthpiece. The Greek playwright, Aristophanes, portrays a considerably different picture of Socrates and truth probably lies as it usually does, somewhere inbetween the two extremes.

Socrates was married, but gossip has it that he was cursed with a nagging wife and felt more comfortable out on the streets than at home. (It's a good thing Athens was blessed with generally good weather!)

He earned his living as a stonecutter, but his real vocation consisted in roaming the *Agora* or marketplace asking tantalizing, yet leading philosophical questions of the citizenry. People regarded him as some sort of a gadfly, a public irritant, albeit for their own good. One might say he was greeted with mixed emotions.

He had a most enquiring mind and never seemed satisfied with the answers he received in response to his questions. Still, he continued "buttonholing" people on the streets. He became a familiar figure and had an interesting approach to people. It always was one of flattery and indirection. It went something like this: Accosting someone he would say,

1

"I've heard some people tell me you're a pretty intelligent person. After all, you've been to school, gotten good grades and are well recommended by your teachers and associates. Would you mind if I, an old ignorant man just trying to learn a few things, would ask you a simple question or two?"

After such a lead-in, how could one refuse? He might respond that Socrates shouldn't believe all that he hears. Nonetheless, the person would try to answer Socrates' questions. How could he do otherwise?

What is Virtue?

Socrates would express a word of thanks and then raise the query, "What is Virtue?" The response probably would be, "Oh! I thought you would have a tough question but that's an easy one. Everyone knows what virtue is. Why there's the virtue of the ruler who governs his people justly, that of the craftsman who skillfully does his job, of the soldier who doesn't flinch in face of the enemy . . . "

At this point, Socrates would shake with excitement and his face shone with delight. It appears, he would say, that he finally found the wise man for which he had been looking all these years. His search was over, but he would ask a few more questions just for some small further clarification. The respondent was kind and perhaps overly generous, for in telling Socrates what virtue was, he gave him an entire list of them.

"Was the respondent telling of the nature of virtue, that is, defining it and declaring what its essence is, or was he only enumerating the various types of virtues, giving a list, but not explaining their common nature?" Socrates' "mentor" now appeared puzzled. Perhaps Socrates hadn't been too clear in his original question. Socrates apologized if this was the case. (It wasn't the case, but Socrates was "killing him with kindness.")

Taken back just a bit, the listener would ask what Socrates meant by the distinction between the *kinds* of virtue and the nature of virtue. Windmills would be tilted for a while and then Socrates would wonder if the interlocutor failed to answer the question directly, choosing instead to make an end run around the issue. In effect, it was clear that there was an attempt to finesse the problem and not address it. Perhaps they had best start from scratch again.

The Socratic Method

At this point the person questioned would admit that maybe he didn't quite know what virtue was, to which Socrates paradoxically enough joyously proclaimed, "Now we're making progress! We've advanced in knowledge at least to the point that we don't know. We have become aware of our ignorance and contrary to appearances, that is a step forward."

What we have just been initiated into is an example of the *Socratic method*. It involved two steps: 1) *irony*, the realization in the learner of his own ignorance, thus clearing the way for the subsequent 2) *maieutic*, the deliverance of the mind enabling it to give birth to truth. Both of these stages were accomplished through a series of questions posed by Socrates, to which the listener would give a conditioned response, thereby arriving at the nature of the problem and the direction of its conclusion. The Socratic method is designed to introduce the mind to a state of *Socratic wisdom* as its new starting point. That is, to know that we don't know, to be aware of our own limitations. When we become Socratically wise, we can then start on the road to truth without being blocked by former prejudices clouding our vision.

As indicated earlier, Socrates wanted to know who was, and then learn from, the wisest man in Athens. This question was put to the Delphic oracle who had a knack for speaking in double *entendres*. The reply was that the wisest man in Athens was—Socrates! What a surprise! But upon reflection, the meaning of this gradually became clear, for Socrates was the only one prepared to search for truth in an unprejudiced way. This was because he started out with being aware of his own ignorance.

Midwifery

Now to seek truth by asking questions meant that one must talk to others, to engage in dialogue. In this respect Socrates compared himself to an old midwife. These were women, who after their own childbearing years were over, or who were unable to bear children in the first place, would assist pregnant women in giving birth. Socrates said he could not generate his own knowledge but that he could help others in giving birth to ideas or concepts.

It is interesting that the process of physical birth and the gathering of knowledge have both mirrored the same language of *conception*. This is hinted at by expressions such as having "intimate knowledge" of the other. Perhaps this is because physical conception and intellectual conception are so precious and so important to mankind.

He acted as a "midwife" then by posing "leading questions," i.e., those with a hint of the answer in them. For example, one might ask a child, "Do you know that two plus two equals four? Let me explain what I mean. Here are 1—2—3—4—blocks. If we take these two here and those two there and put them together we have—let's count together—1—2—3—4. Now do you know that two plus two equals four?" The child will answer "Yes." It appears to the casual observer that Socrates was drawing knowledge out of the child, knowledge that the child didn't know he already had in his own mind. The child was perceptive enough to "get the answer," but not perceptive enough to know that implicitly, Socrates was "giving the answer" in the question. This style of teaching is called "Socratic teaching," and is highly effective when properly handled. Students often are saved considerable embarrassment over other methods that attempt to expose their limited knowledge or ignorance in direct fashion. They also are well pleased with themselves!

Trouble Ahead

As Socrates kept up this practice of interrogating others, many became angry at having their egos pricked and resentment began to set in against Socrates. This grew as Socrates attracted many of the younger set who delighted in seeing their highly respected elders "put down" by this old man.

Eventually, the ruling class became so upset that they trumped up charges against Socrates and brought him to trial. The charges were two: impiety to the gods (they were still a handy tool to have around) and the corruption of youth, i.e., they began to poke fun at the Established Order, always a dangerous practice. Socrates' defense at his trial, which is given in Plato's *The Apology*, was philosophically sound but he was ruled guilty and sentenced to death. The court offered him exile instead for they only wanted to get rid of him, but no self respecting Greek would choose that. After all, the State was one's mother and father. One's own identity was intimately tied up with the State, so much so did the Athenians pride themselves on being Athenian Greeks. Without the State, the non-citizen was in effect a non-person.

So it was that Socrates drank the poisonous hemlock in his jail cell. So it was that the Athenians sinned against Philosophy. And so it was that the world lost one of its greatest moral thinkers. He died but his ideas lived on. They were preserved and extended by his student, Plato.

SOCRATES

Review Questions

1. What is your own personal reaction to a gadfly, that is, to a person who would like to help you improve yourself, for your own good, of course?
2. See if you can "make a case" for some kind of ignorance as being intimately involved in every act that is morally bad.
3. What does it mean to be "Socratically wise?"
4. What was Socrates specifically looking for when he interrogated people?
5. Do you think your relationship to the State is similiar to that of the ancient Greeks, especially Socrates? Why or why not?

Special Thought Question

Should Socrates have accepted his death sentence, when he could have been given a lesser punishment? What was the principle involved in his choice and could this be interpreted as a martyrdom complex?

BIBLIOGRAPHY

Primary Source: Socrates never wrote, but Plato gives us many of his basic ideas through the *Dialogues*. Most germane here are Plato's *Apology, Phaedo,* and perhaps *Lysis.* Each is readily available in a number of editions.

Secondary Source: *Socrates: The Original and Its Image.* Alan Blum (London: Routledge & K. Paul, 1978). A thorough review of the man and the myth.

2

PLATO (428–347 B.C.)

"False words are not only evil in themselves, but they infect the soul with evil." Phaedo

The Birth of Idealism

Plato is probably the best known and least understood of all philosophers. He was aptly eulogized by the contemporary philosopher-mathematician, Alfred North Whitehead, when the latter declared, "All Western Philosophy is but a footnote to Plato."

I don't believe it was Plato's solutions to the problems which has given him that stature; rather it was his *raising* of nearly all of the great problems of philosophy. In short, more than most men, Plato was able to ask the intelligent questions. Now, as we know, it is not an easy thing to ask a truly meaningful question, for one must already know part of the answer to do so. For example, what question could one raise in higher mathematics, or nuclear physics, over which men for generations would rack their brains? Obviously, one would have to know the fields quite well before one would be able to raise such questions. Well, so it was with Plato. The questions which he introduced are still with us and we have not yet plumbed their depths.

Plato's Life and Times

But before we go into some of these questions, let's take a look at the life of Plato and the times in which he lived. Knowing something about the man and his environment will show us that Plato was not simply an abstract thinker but a practical person, a man who like ourselves also was made of flesh and blood.

Plato lived in Athens, Greece, almost twenty-five centuries ago, being born about 428 B.C. He died when he was about eighty years old.

For the most part, Greek culture (paideia) was polytheistic, that is, they believed in many gods. The Olympian religion was the official religion in the century during which Plato was born. We're familiar with the names of their various gods—Zeus, king of them all, Athena, goddess of philosophy who sprung out of Zeus' head, Poseidon, god of the sea, Hygeia, goddess of health, etc. Later, many of the Romans accepted these gods also but gave them different names. For example, Zeus became Jupiter, Poseidon became Neptune, Hermes became Mercury, and so on. It was all confusing and so concerned were the Greeks that somewhere along the line, they may have missed out on a god, they made a statue to the "unknown god," just in case! Well, who can argue? It's always good to be on the safe side.

By Plato's time, however, fear of the gods had pretty well ended, especially among the intellectuals, and religion was reduced largely to being a mere formality. Yet the gods were always there in the background, as witness what happened to Socrates. The philosophers like to pride themselves that they were able to break out of a previous anthropomorphism, i.e., the notion that gods have the characteristics of men, good and bad. These intellectuals looked more and more to reason as the explanation for things rather than myth and religion. Nonetheless, the change was more gradual than abrupt.

Plato grew up in these challenging and changing times. He was of royal descent and his own relatives were members of the ruling class of Athens. This well may be one of the reasons why Plato always had such an intense interest in politics, ("political philosophy," if we want to dress up that word).

Plato's early years coincided with the Peloponnesian War which finally resulted in breaking the hold of Athens as ruler of the Mediterranean. The political life of the times was extremely turbulent. In Athens, democracy ended in a veritable mob rule. At the close of the war, a group of men, some of whom were Plato's own kin, took over the government and ruled with such bloodshed and oppression that this period came to be known as the "Rule of the Thirty Tyrants." After seeing both the aristocratic and democratic forms of government fail miserably, Plato gave up any idea he may have entertained about entering the field of Athenian government. Instead, he taught and traveled and eventually drew up an ideal State which he set forth in his best known work, *The Republic*. Here he discusses the various duties of the citizens of the State and compares the divisions of the State to the types of virtues.

What is Virtue?

But let's backtrack for a moment. We recall that Socrates' chief concern was the nature of virtue. That concern came out of the basic moral question, "Why do we do wrong?" It was the same question early Christians, such as St. Paul and St. Augustine raised, "Why do we do what we would not do, and why do we not do what we would?" This seems to be a common practice as well as a common problem for us all. The Socratic-Platonic answer is quite different from the Christian answer. The latter explains the reason for man's moral wrong-doing to be the offshoot of sin and a fallen nature, coupled to a weakened will. This however is not the response found in Plato who maintains a thoroughly intellectualist position. It is a fascinating one and we gravitate both toward his explanation as well as away from it.

Very simply, Plato claims that the reason we don't do what is right is because we don't really know what is right. After all, doesn't it seem impossible to claim that man can *knowingly* act contrary to his own good? Isn't there an element of ignorance in every wrongful action— perhaps ignorance of the consequences this action may bring us?

Let's take an example. A man plans to rob a bank, but upon getting there discovers police everywhere, both inside and outside of the bank. Someone has tipped them off as to the planned robbery. Obviously, he won't rob the bank at this time because he *knows for sure* that he will be caught. His knowing prevented him from robbing the bank. He will do so only when he thinks through ignorance that perhaps he won't be caught. This comes down to the view that virtue is knowledge and therefore that vice is a form of ignorance. If this is the case, then how might the world rid itself of vice and wrongful action? The clear answer seems to be through gaining more knowledge for everyone—through education (and that is why education plays such an important role in the State for Plato.) Even today when a highly educated person commits a crime, we are much more aghast than if a poor and uneducated person does. We ask ourselves of the educated person, "How could he do such a thing? He's smart, so it doesn't make sense?" With respect to the uneducated, we may shrug our shoulders and claim that perhaps he *didn't know any better.*

This argument seems sound enough at first, but let's check it out with our experiences. It seems we can know a thing is bad for us and *still* do it. How many M.D.'s for example, continue to be heavy cigarette smokers? Or how many heavy set people know they should diet but don't? Plato would answer that they really don't know, that is, as a matter of absolute conviction, that this is wrong or bad. This *conviction* is a very special kind of knowledge that differs qualitatively from the ordinary way the term "knowledge" is used. Put this way, Plato has a point, and yet one might ask how many of us are capable of such absolute conviction and can direct our emotions and passions to go along with reason. One can see why Plato's position here is called intellectualistic. For most of us, we are not pure minds like *Star Trek's* Mr. Spock. We are fallible creatures of flesh and blood. Nonetheless the idealism of Plato is a worthy goal to shoot for. In fact as we get older and the drives of the passions are lessened, we do tend more and more to follow reason or common sense.

On this overall problem Plato paints a picture in which we can all recognize ourselves. Man, he says, is like a man driving a chariot with a two horse rig. One horse (paralleling the irascible appetite of man) wants to go one way, while the other (the concupiscible appetite) strives to go in an opposite direction. The man driving the chariot (reason) has all he can handle to direct the two contrary horses to the direction of his goal as driver. He needs the horses (passions or appetites) to get where he wants to go, but the driver (reason) must always keep them under control. As a side remark to this weighty issue, cf. the cynic, Voltaire, an Enlightenment wit. Most men, says Voltaire, consider themselves becoming virtuous after the age of forty, when in fact they are only suffering a loss of energy!

Virtue in Man and the State

Getting back to the larger issue of virtue, then, where are we to look for it? Well, if one wishes to understand the skill of carpentry, one goes to observe a carpenter at work. So it is with virtue. The way to study it would be to observe those men others consider virtuous. Now there is no need to study virtue in the individual man, when we can more easily examine it as magnified in the State. After all, the State is the collective man, or MAN writ large. This, then, is where Plato commences his inquiry.

According to Plato, the State exhibits three basic divisions or classes of citizens. Each class will be characterized by its own specific talent or virtue. These divisions are 1) The Ruler, who guides the State; 2) The Soldier-Police, who guard the State and ensure order; and 3) The Merchant-Citizens, i.e., artists and craftsmen, who carry on the day to day commercial and industrial activities.

What we expect and find in the good Ruler is that he acts with practical wisdom. Hence in him the virtue of *prudence* predominates. The soldier-police need *courage* above all else, and the merchant-citizens need *temperance*.

We will note that we now have discovered three of the four cardinal virtues required both of the good State and the good man. (The reason they are called "cardinal" is because "cardinal" means "hinge" and they are the key virtues on which all others hinge.) The missing virtue in the above is *justice*, and it essentially is composite, for it will be present when all of the parts of the State are working harmoniously, each performing well its proper function.

This analogy of the State and the cardinal virtues may now be brought to bear on the individual man, for similar divisions abound there. In man, the head is the ruling part (prudence), the heart or irascible appetite should be strong (courage), and the stomach (concupiscible appetite) should be moderate in its wants (temperance). When these three virtues are present, a harmony (justice) will be present. The key to all of the virtues, of course, is prudence. To possess it is to have the others, for a man who is prudent cannot be also intemperate, unjust, etc. In this sense, as indicated earlier, all virtue is a kind of *knowing* what is the right thing to be and to do. This knowing of the right, will ensure doing what is right, i.e., acting virtuously. Yet this will be true only if such knowledge is a matter of absolute conviction. It follows then that if the philosopher is the most knowledgeable person, it is he who should be king and who will lead people and the State to be virtuous.

Plato the Educator

When Plato was about 40 years old, he bought a house and started what was probably the first university in the Western world. The man from whom he purchased the building was named *Academus* and Plato's school, therefore, became known as the *Academy*. Mathematics and political science were the two principal subjects taught, yet these took in a wide variety of topics that in our time would be covered under separate disciplines. One of his illustrious pupils there was Aristotle.

Today, we can learn of Plato's ideas by browsing through a large number of his authored works called "Dialogues." They constitute his popular writings, his technical ones having been lost through time. They read more like conversations than textbooks and their beauty and style have yet to be imitated successfully. Most are short in length. In them, Plato uses some well known figure as his chief speaker, who, in turn, carries on a conversation with others about some important issue. Generally, the leading character is Socrates, Plato's early teacher. There is often a central theme to each dialogue. The *Lysis* treats of friendship, the *Phaedo*, of immortality, the *Meno*, of man's preexistence in another world, etc.

Emulating Socrates, the pattern of the dialogue is to raise questions about a set of related problems and examine tentative answers, all of which are found wanting in some respect. Yet the rejection of each answer also hints at another path to be taken as we laboriously work our way toward truth. Seldom is a firm and definitive answer given. Instead, the reader is encouraged to make up his own mind on the issue. This technique reveals Plato was a master teacher who provides directions without getting in the way of the reader's efforts at philosophizing.

On occasion, one finds certain inconsistencies in the "Dialogues," due primarily to the fact that the writings reflect the gradual development of Plato's thought. The "Dialogues" written early in his career reflect more the issues of interest to his mentor, Socrates. Those written at a later period in life concern themselves more with Plato's own political philosophy and views on the nature of law.

The Nature of Man

A pivotal point in any philosophy is how it construes the nature of man. What is man? Is he nothing but matter? Is he fundamentally mind or soul or is he some combination of these? If the latter, how do these combine? Do they unite as a rider and a horse or say a pilot and his ship. If so, each can get off at any time and go its own way, especially the rider, and sometimes not through his own choice! The latter unity of parts is termed an aggregate or *accidental unity*. On the other hand, in a chemical compound such as water, we experience an *essential* or substantial unity. Water is not H_2O strictly speaking, for water puts out fires while hydrogen and oxygen only fuel them. Water comes to be as a "third thing" —something different than its parts. It has its own specific properties. In water, the parts have lost their own identity to become one with the whole. This is not true of horse and rider.

According to Plato, in this life, man basically is a soul enclosed in a body dragged down by the world as an oyster in its shell. He seems to suggest punishment for some wrongdoing as responsible for this condition. The soul longs to go back to the world of ideas from which it came. It is immortal. The present union between body and soul in man is an accidental union such as a rider and a horse—like a chemical colloid (where parts retain their identity as in a mixture of oil and water) instead of the substantial unity as in a chemical compound. The *real* man is the soul and this is why it receives first priority in Plato's philosophy. This notion of man is quite common to the Western world and has been assimilated by many religions. The question must be raised again however, "How does it stack up with one's own experience?" This is always the ultimate philosophical court.

If one goes to a funeral and asks "Did my friend die or did his body die?," those in the Platonic tradition, would say, his body died. But doesn't this go counter to all that we experience? What we see is that our friend who was alive, now is no more. He is dead. Whether a part of him is immortal is a separate question, unless by "our friend" we meant his

11

soul. This of course is Plato's position. But it certainly is not the way we speak and act. Is the "I" only the soul or is it the result of the soul-body union, like water the result of H$_2$O? Does my *hand* (body) write a letter? Does my *soul* write a letter? Or do "I" write a letter? Is the body an essential or an accidental part of mÿ self? For Plato, who is into a rather spiritualist tradition on this point, the body is accidental rather than essential to man. Playing on words, one might ask another how he *feels* about this.

Sense vs. Intellectual Knowledge

Much of Plato's philosophy centers around his views on the nature of knowledge. Let's see if we can come to grips with some of the problems Plato suggests to us on these matters.

In the dialogue, *Timaeus*, Plato asks a question which at first looks like double talk. "What is that which is always becoming and never is?", he inquires, and "What is that which always is but is never becoming?"

What prompted such questions was the fact that man seems to have two kinds of knowledge. There is *sensory* knowledge which is always changing, because the sensory world, its object, is continually in flux or change. For example, the shadow a tree casts is different at morning, noon and night. The clouds we see are always moving and changing shapes.

Sense knowledge deals with what is accidental, changeable, phenomenal. In short, it deals with appearances of things, not with reality. It is not *really* worthy to be called knowledge. Rather, suggests Plato, let us call *opinion* and *belief* the state of mind which deals with such things as the changeable sensible world in which we presently live.

But over and above this sensory knowledge, we do grasp some things which are unchanging and eternal. When we know something true, it is true for all time. For example, what is a courageous act will always win acclaim. The fact that 2 + 2 = 4 was always so—all men have basically the same unchanging nature. This is *intellectual* knowledge and it is the *only* knowledge worthy of the name. It concerns itself with what is unchanging, and essential. That we are capable of such lofty heights as attaining this knowledge, Plato never doubted for a moment. But the problem had to be explained as to how we could come to have intellectual knowledge. It doesn't seem to be derived from the sensory order of things. After all, true knowledge is so different from changing sensible opinion.

Now, Plato argued, if there is a real order of things which corresponds to our sensory knowledge, namely the world in which we live, so there should be an even more real order of things which corresponds to our intellectual knowledge. Such a world, could be called a world of ideas, a world of essences or forms, as they were known. Different from the sensory order of things, it was much more real. In fact, the sensory world is but a participation and reflection, a poor imitation of the world of ideas. One might say analogously as a shadow is to the tree which casts it, the sense world is to the world of ideas. As one can see, Plato not only goes out of his way to explain things, he goes out of this world to do so! It is in this sense that Plato's philosophy may be termed an idealism, for it favors the reality of ideas over that of the sensory world. Since in some way he holds for two realms of reality, he may also be called a dualist.

From where and what do we get our intellectual knowledge and truth then? Not from the sensory world, but rather from the intelligible world of essences or ideas. This meant for Plato, that somehow we must have been in contact with such a world in a previous existence. That is why Plato held for the transmigration of souls (metempsychois) and for our coming into this life with ideas which are inborn or *innate*. We merely have to be stimulated to remember these. Hence, for Plato, *knowing in this life* is really a case of being stimulated to *remembering* what we learned in a previous existence. Analogously again, as a shadow can remind us of the tree, the sense world recollects for us the higher world of ideas.

To the question, then, "What is always becoming but never is?", the answer is the sense world, for it is always changing and is never the same. To the question, "What is that which always is but is never becoming?", the answer is the world of essences, the world of ideas, the world of being, the world of truth. It is the aim of the essential part of man, his soul, to go back to this realm of ideas after death.

Above this divine world of essences, there is what some have called the Platonic god, whom Plato calls the GOOD or the ONE. Harking back to our analogy, it is ultimately like the sun which gives the light by which the tree casts the shadow. In the *Republic*, Plato expresses these thoughts in the well known "Allegory of the Cave," and the "simile of the divided line."

Allegory of the Cave

Let us take a brief look at the allegory of the cave. Plato is great at telling stories and he asks us to imagine some human beings deep in a cave chained to a wall there since birth. They face the rear of the cave and are unable to turn in any direction except to stare at the rear of the cave. Now on the other side of the wall (which the prisoners cannot see) there is a fire and other persons who carry statues of horses, trees, etc. on their heads and walk between the fire and the wall. They talk to each other. As they walk by the wall, the flickering fire casts an ever changing shadow of the statues (their own bodies hidden by the six foot wall) on the back of the cave. This is seen by the prisoners. Because the cave has an echo, the prisoners think that the images which they see are reality itself and they attribute the echo of the voices to the images themselves.

Now one of the prisoners breaks his bonds and climbs over the wall. Suddenly he realizes that the shadows were not what is real, but thinks statues are the reality. He deduces that the shadows were themselves visible only by virtue of the light of the fire. Further, the statues do not talk, the men do. The prisoners see only appearances (which are deceptive); he observes reality. Still not satisfied though, he eventually works his way out of the cave and enters the world above at night. There he sees real trees, the moon and so forth. He thinks these now are the "really real." But when day comes he sees things as they really are and comes to know that the sun is the highest principle of reality in which everything else participates for its own limited reality. He knows this because he sees that the tree depends for its life on the sun, but not vice versa. Armed with such knowledge, he goes back to the cave to enlighten his fellow prisoners that what they grasp is only appearance. He has seen reality and will lead them to it. Because of his sudden descent into the darkness of the cave, however, his eyes used to the sunlight are temporarily blinded and within the cave itself, he cannot even see the shadows he formerly knew. The prisoners now scoff at him and if he continues to claim that he has the truth they may do him in. The analogy to Socrates is too obvious to be missed. At any rate, by means of this analogy, Plato tries to show again that reality is a two tiered world. It is the second tier which is important. Through it we are led to the dwelling place of the Sun—the One—the Good.

Plato's Influence

Because Plato sometimes wrote obscurely and often used myths to express his ideas, he is open to various interpretations. Perhaps this partially accounts for his fame. Indeed, some early writers in the Church thought that just as Moses was given revealed truths by God for the Jews, Plato was given revealed truths by God for the Gentiles. Certainly, Plato does speak about a fall of man, about a great flood covering the earth, about Atlantis, about a god who is good and who is a creator. Yet the similarities to be the Judeo-Christian Biblical history on these points can be explained in other ways.

For thirteen centuries after the birth of Christ, Plato continued to exercise predominant influence on the Western world, largely under the qualified patronage of St. Augustine. Plato's philosophy opened the door to mysticism for many in the West for although it was intellectualist, it embodied elements of a moral and religious nature as well. In this sense, the role of the philosopher is to lead others from our earthy den of semi-darkness to the world of truth and light.

Even in our own day and age, we often continue to think Platonically, as though *man is his soul*, as though *virtue is knowledge*, and as though *education is the cure-all* for the ills of society. Plato died about twenty-three centuries ago, but many continue to turn to him for his provocative questions and tentative answers to the meaning of life.

PLATO

Review Questions

1. Was Plato a commoner or aristocrat and approximately when did he live?
2. In general, what was the political mood of the times? Stability or change, and why?
3. Show how Question 2 had a bearing on Plato producing the utopian book, *The Republic?*
4. What are the four cardinal virtues and how does Plato relate them to the State and to the individual?
5. Regarding Question 4, which does he analyze first, the State or the individual? Why?
6. Specifically, why is education so important for Plato in attempting to resolve the nature of virtue?
7. Plato has a two-tier theory of knowledge. The one corresponds to "what is always becoming but never is,"; the other is "what always is and is never becoming." What are these two orders?
8. How do the above two orders in Question 7 relate to each other?
9. How did Plato argue to man's previous existence?
10. What is the parallel between the physical sun and the Good?

Special Thought Question

Can a person knowingly act contrary to his own good?

BIBLIOGRAPHY

Primary Source: *The Works of Plato,* Ed. by Irwin Edmon (New York: Modern Library, c. 1928). (This is a popular selection of Plato's major works.)

Secondary Source: *The Death of Socrates.* Romano Guardini. Tr. by B. Wrighton (Cleveland: World Publishing Co., 1962). (An analysis of four dialogues of Plato.)

3
ARISTOTLE (384–322 B.C.)

"All men by nature desire to know." Metaphysics

A Return to Realism

Seldom in history do two great figures follow directly upon one another in the same country. Greatness usually brings with it a gap or hiatus before another famous person emerges. A notable exception to this, of course, was the following of Plato upon Socrates. Still more notable, however, is a man who studied under Plato and to whom Plato referred as "The Mind" and "The Reader." Later, in the Middle Ages this "Reader" was universally known as THE PHILOSOPHER. He discovered and formulated the laws of the science of logic and fathered countless sciences. He enumerated the basic laws of association in psychology, gave the classic definition to tragedy, presented the clearest treatise yet written on virtue, set down basic demonstrations for the existence of a supreme being, and argued that it is befitting man's dignity to study such lowly things as worms. His name was Aristotle.

Scientist, Teacher, Philosopher

Oddly enough, many have not heard of the name of Aristotle, yet, Aristotle has probably influenced Western civilization more than any other human person. Aristotle lived about twenty-three centuries ago. He was born in 384 B.C. on the northern coast of the Aegean Sea, in a city now known as Stavro. His father was a doctor and had as one of his patients, the king of Macedonia, who was the grandfather of the world conqueror, Alexander the Great. For a short time, Aristotle served as Alexander's teacher.

Aristotle was extremely interested in biology and possibly practiced medicine himself. Later, he went to Athens and studied under Plato for nearly twenty years. After Plato died, Aristotle became disgusted with the school's administration and change of orientation and traveled to some of the Greek colonies. Eventually he returned to Athens and set up his own school, which, in objectives, was not dissimilar to present day universities.

Although a Greek, Aristotle was an alien to the city-state of Athens. Consequently, he could only rent the buildings which housed his school called the Lyceum. Apparently, Aristotle often would instruct his students while walking around the garden. Hence, his group and those who followed his teachings, became known as the Peripatetics, which means literally, *to walk around.*

Fortunately, Aristotle had quite a windfall in money given him by Alexander the Great. This helped Aristotle set up a model school. At the time, it was the greatest center of universal learning. Scientific research was carried on, libraries were created, political constitutions were collected and evaluated, and, in general, all of the normal scholarly activities were supported for an elitist student body.

Like his teacher, Plato, Aristotle wrote two kinds of works, namely, highly technical books for his students as well as rather popular dialogues for the educated Greek. But just the opposite happened to Aristotle's writings as occurred to Plato's. Aristotle's popular works were lost and the technical ones remained extant. This might be one reason why Plato (whose own set of *Dialogues*), unlike Aristotle, is so well known to the average person. After all, Plato is fun to read. In fact one can read Plato, not understand him and still enjoy him. Reading Aristotle, however, is usually painstaking, although the rewards are great.

A Grasp of Essentials

Aristotle had an unusual capacity for summing up a situation with near absolute precision. You may recall that Athens was invaded by a group of men known as *Sophists.* These were travelling teachers, poets and dilettanti. They took money for their teaching, an unusual procedure for the time, although that is not the reason why both Plato and Aristotle condemned them. It was their relativism and pragmatism (the view that truth is what works) that irked Aristotle and Plato. They denied an interest in absolute truth. Two of the more famous, immortalized in the names of two separate *Dialogues* of Plato, were Protagoras and Gorgias. It is to the former that we attribute the saying, "Man is the measure of all things," in effect, everything is relative to how we look at it. This view is immensely popular in our own time, but then it was almost a scandal. They sought in the expression of the American philosopher, William James, the "bitch goddess of success."

Among other things, they taught young men how to be lawyers and win their cases by fair means or foul. Aristotle describes them simply as "having the appearance of knowledge without the reality." If this is what a Sophist was, we might question when a person says that we're sophisticated, whether he is insulting or complimenting us! Today, however, scholars agree that both Plato and Aristotle were a bit heavyhanded in their critique of the Sophists. These teachers did serve certain real needs.

Aristotle's capacity for precision again is reflected in his definition of scientific knowledge as "when we know the cause on which the fact depends, as the cause of that fact and no other, and further, that the fact could not be other than it is." What he is saying in such truncated fashion is that to be scientific, knowledge must deal with causes and be necessary rather than happenstance. What is studied *must* happen in that way because of the relation of cause and effect which is the object of enquiry. Accordingly, scientific truth will be universal and necessary, that is, good for all time. On this, Aristotle is a rigorist, allowing no exception. As an example of the clear thinking which science demands, Aristotle would raise the following kind of issue. Is this (white, granular thing before me) sugar because it is sweet? Or is it sweet because it is sugar? What's the difference one might say? Simply this, "sweet" and "sugar" are causally related but in different respects. Tasting this to determine it is "sweet" is the cause of our *knowing* it is sugar. In fact, however, it is "sweet" because it is sugar. The first is the cause of our knowing; the second of the thing being so, i.e., sweetness derives from sugar and not vice versa. There's something to think about!

Another instance of his quest for precision is his definition of Tragedy as "the imitation of an action that is serious and also, as having magnitude, complete in itself; in language with pleasurable accessories, each kind brought in separately in the parts of the work; in a dramatic, not in a narrative form; with incidents arousing pity and fear, wherewith to accomplish its catharsis of such emotions." Shakespeare's *King Lear* and *Othello* are clear embodiments of this definition. Consider only the classic line from *Othello*, the noble Moor, "Speak of me as one who has loved, not too wisely, but too well!"

Almost always, tragedy involves a great person with a small defect. Over time the small defect (character fault) becomes larger and larger, eventually doing in the great person. In Othello's case, the defect was a spark of jealousy, fueled by Iago to become a raging self destructive fire.

Departure from Athens

Although Aristotle lived many years in Athens, he did not remain there to the time he died. We may recall that Alexander the Great died in Babylon in 323 B.C. Well, it seems that Athens had been getting nervous about the intentions of the Macedonian war-machine and Alexander's death triggered off a good deal of anti-Macedonian sentiment. Aristotle, who had Macedonian ties, began to be regarded very suspiciously by some of the Athenians. This was rather ridiculous for Aristotle never sympathized with the Alexandrian views of merging Greek and Persian culture. Like most Greeks, Aristotle regarded the Persians as barbarians. As a matter of fact, one of Aristotle's nephews was executed on the grounds of conspiracy against Alexander. Still, the Athenians were making known their unhappiness with Aristotle's presence.

Aristotle was subtle enough to take the hint and left town in a hurry, "Lest," as he is reputed to have said, "the Greeks sin twice against philosophy." The first time the Greeks sinned against Philosophy, of course, was when they put Socrates to death. Aristotle died at the age of 62. He suffered from some kind of stomach ailment, probably aggravated by excessive study. His love for study was so great that the story has it, when reading for many hours, he would hold a brass ball in his hand. If he fell asleep, the ball would drop and awaken him by its noise. It is no exaggeration to say that his entire life was spent seeking knowledge in which he regarded human perfection was to be found.

Aristotelian Realism

Although Aristotle's teacher, Plato, was an idealist, the mature Aristotle was a realist, a "philosopher of common sense." Plato we recall, held that we are born with ideas from another world. Aristotle, on the contrary, maintained that there is nothing in the mind which did not first come through the senses, so that all knowledge has the sensory order as its source. Thus, at first, the intellect of man is like a blank tablet, according to Aristotle, and we spend our lives trying to fill it in. In short, there are no innate ideas and no separate world of Platonic ideas. What we come to know is entirely from this world. If whatever imput we have in the mind is from this world, then it is obvious that the better our senses function, the greater opportunity we have for intellectual development, all things considered, e.g., discipline for study, etc.

Some senses grasp the same thing in common. For example, I can tell that an object is round by looking at it, or by feeling it with my eyes closed. Other aspects of objects, however, can be known by one sense and that sense alone. Take color, for example. How would one try to explain the difference between yellow and red to a person who was blind from birth. There is no way this could be done in any meaningful sense. Even explaining the spectrum would be of no help. And yet, to see the difference is simplicity itself, we have but to open our eyes. One can truly marvel at the remarkable Helen Keller, who reached such high intellectual development despite having been deprived of sight, speech and hearing!

Aristotle did agree with Plato that there is a qualitative difference between sensory and intellectual knowledge. In brief, while Aristotle was no idealist (ideas didn't exist outside the mind for him as they did for Plato), he was an intellectualist. The grounds for this was not the reality of two different worlds (Plato) but two different ways of man being able to grasp the one world in which he lives. Our intellect, claims Aristotle, is able to know the same object grasped by the sense, but the intellect, through its own proper activity of abstraction and intellection, is able to know the object in its essential character. In looking at a man, for example, the senses grasp the facts of his height, color of skin, weight, etc. The intellect apprehends much more, namely the fact that here is a rational animal. The intellect knows this through intuition and inferences or both, activities that the senses do not possess. Analogously, the mind is something like an X-ray machine. With naked vision we only see the outside covering of a human body. With an X-ray, we can penetrate to the internal parts and see the bone structure, etc. The structure was there all along, but not available to the naked eye. This, then, is like the difference between what the senses grasp and what the intellect can apprehend.

These activities of mind suggest that in some way, it is or contains an immaterial (spiritual?) nature. (This point, although not elaborated by Aristotle, is developed considerably in the Middle Ages.)

Unlike Plato, who saw man as "a soul imprisoned in a body," Aristotle viewed body and soul as complementary, they are naturally united to form one being, the substance, man. Also unlike Plato, Aristotle, the medical student saw that humans die. This was an essential and not an accidental change. It also is in agreement with our own observation and experience. It shows once more Aristotle the realist.

A World of Order and Purpose

Perhaps because of his biological training, Aristotle saw the world and things in it as purposive (*teleological*). He saw things as acting for ends, rather than by chance. Different things have different goals and various objects in motion seek their natural place. Of course, Aristotle's theory of natural place and movement is basically wrong (as shown by contemporary physics). He held that for a stone to fall from one's hand upon release was a *natural* movement, gravitating earthward as it does. To throw it upward is an unnatural motion of the stone. When it reaches the apex of its flight it reverts to its natural gravitational motion once again. Such a theory could not explain present day satellites in orbit. Despite this, most of us can agree with his overview that nature acts for some kind of purpose. In a human organism, the eyelids serve as a dust protector for the eyes, the nose hairs (cilia) serve as a filter, and the body tends to adjust itself to fit its own needs. Although contemporary biologists don't like this method of explanation, it does fit our common experience. And to a large extent, this was Aristotle's forte, to explain such a world of common sense.

To make science possible, things in the universe could be categorized and explained in terms of four basic causes, all of which admit of further refinement. These are: 1) the *material cause* or that out of which a thing comes to be. E.g., the wood out of which a chair is fashioned. 2) the *formal cause* or that determining principle which makes matter to be this rather than something else. E.g., the shape or form of the chair when given to the wood makes that wood to be a chair rather than having the shape or form of a desk. 3) the *efficient cause* or the agent through whose activity the form comes to determine the matter. E.g., the carpenter. 4) the *final cause* or that for the sake of which the agent acts. E.g., the chair is produced to have something for people to sit upon. By using these causes, we now had intellectual tools for defining things with precision and such tools are rigorously employed in his work on logic. As an incidental it should be mentioned that Aristotle was the first to develop such a system of formal logic and it put order into thinking.

The Nature of Reality

Everything in the material world, then, consists of two basic principles which complement each other, namely matter and form (the material and formal cause). This theory is termed hylemorphism.

Looking at reality at large, rather than just material reality, Aristotle asks what is the nature of "being." What is it that makes things to be real? Such questions belong to the realm of metaphysics, but the answers are consistent with his matter and form theory of the physical world.

"Being" in its most basic meaning is substance. All reality or being is ultimately some combination of potency and act (such as matter and form) or act alone. By potency generally is meant a capacity for determination or perfection; act is the perfection itself. In art, for example, the rough block of marble has the *potentiality* to be shaped into an *actual* likeness of David by the sculptor, Michaelangelo. Once given this, it is a perfected work of art. In many ways, argues Aristotle, art is both an imitation and perfection of nature. We see this today especially in the medical art of surgery.

What is difficult to grasp is that for Aristotle, potency is not an actuality but is still a principle of reality. It is less than something and more than nothing. For example, the capacity a man has for playing the violin is more than nothing, yet it isn't anything actual until we find him actually playing the violin.

The important insight of reality as constituted of potency and act, or act alone, enabled Aristotle to solve the problem of the nature of motion, (dynamic activity which is always partly in potency and partly in act; more technically put, "the act of a being in potency insofar as it is in potency"). In effect, whatever is in motion is undergoing a perpetual infusion of newness, which can only be explained by something else providing that newness. The principle which governs this then necessitates that "whatever is moved, is moved by another."

With the principles of potency and act, Aristotle could now explain why there is a plurality of things in the world and why within the same species, there could be any number of individuals each claiming the same nature, e.g., individual humans equally belonging to mankind. He also could argue from beings that were complex unities to a being which was a simple unity and was their explanation. From moved movers, he could argue to an unmoved mover, sometimes called a prime mover. Aristotle characterized the first prime mover as "self thinking thought." It was also known as "Pure Act." In effect this supreme being was the Aristoteliam God and Christians later so identified it and built a theology on its concept. It is fair to say, however, that Aristotle's God, unlike the Christian God, was not providential, nor one who loves. At best, its thought was inner rather than outer directed and it was impersonal. We can see then it is a far cry from Yaweh of the Jewish-Christian tradition.

Politics

Politically, Aristotle pointed out that what is best in theory, is sometimes not the best in practice. Thus, rule of one, where all power is vested in the hands of a benevolent dictator, while theoretically the best way to get things done, in practice is too subject to abuse, man's nature being what it is. Although it was many centuries before Lord Acton lived, Aristotle recognized that "all power corrupts and absolute power corrupts absolutely." Hence, although in theory, rule by many is a very weak kind of rule and unity, it is often better in practice. Such governments are more difficult to overthrow, for the power is so well distributed, whereas, in a dictatorship, if we get rid of one man, generally the government is overthrown. We might argue thus for a strong middle class and their participation in government if we wish a strong foundation for the state.

Virtue and Happiness

As it is natural for men to wonder and wish to know (which explains the origin and quest for philosophy), it is also natural that men seek happiness in all that they do. We cannot but seek happiness, although we may be mistaken in what we consider will make us happy. True happiness is not to be found in the life of pleasure but the life of virtue, for virtue involves striving toward and acquisition of the real good. Hence, we must distinguish between satisfaction, contentment, pleasure, joy and true happiness. Because Aristotle sought absolute happiness, his ethics has been termed *eudaemonistic*, that is, tending toward happiness.

Broadly speaking, there are two kinds of virtues: 1) those which perfect the intellect, such as science and wisdom, and 2) those which perfect the will, that is, the moral virtues of courage, justice, temperance, etc.

For Aristotle, man's perfection lies in the perfection of his highest power, the intellect. Hence, intellectual contemplation of what is highest in being can be termed the supreme good for man.

Yet man needs good habits of the will to live the ordered life necessary for achieving his end. And here, with the moral virtues, Aristotle has given us some valuable insights. Such virtues, he says, are always a "mean" or middle ground between two extremes, which he terms "excess" and "defect."

As an example, we may take courage or bravery. It is the middle ground between foolhardiness (the excess) and cowardice (the defect). Modesty is the middle ground between shamelessness and bashfulness. Now the question arises, "Is the middle ground the same for all, or does it differ with various individuals?" In short, is the mean objective and absolute or subjective and relative?

Aristotle points out that with some virtues the mean is subjective— what is excessive for one might not be so for another, for example, in eating or drinking. What is a big meal for a thin person doing office work might be a small one for a person who is a lumberjack. On the other hand, some virtues have an objective mean which is the same for all. Take the matter of justice, which is the virtue of giving to another his due. Here, all who are just, must give the same to the other, namely whatever is his due. One can give more than what is due, but this no longer is justice but magnanimity. It is interesting too that although virtue lies in moderation, that is, the middle ground between excess and defect, the *practice* of virtue should never be moderate.

Influence

The influence of Aristotelian thought was first felt in the Arab world whose scholars obtained manuscripts unavailable to the Latin West. The Arabs were particularly enamoured with Aristotelian science. They were gifted in astronomy, mathematics and medicine. In the high Middle Ages, however, Aristotle's philosophy and science burst upon Christianity and has remained its leading non-Christian influence. Cardinal Newman sums up the spirit of this influence when he declared, "All men are Aristotelians, whether they will it or no, for in a sense, Aristotle spoke for the entire human race."

Today, many scientists complain that the influence and authority of Aristotle was so strong that the new and contemporary science was held back from development for nearly three hundred years. There is truth in this statement as we see in Church attitudes toward Galileo.

It must be acknowledged that in science, rather than in metaphysics, Aristotle was locked into a limited model which eventually was to go the way of the dodo bird. As one philosopher put it, "Aristotle's astronomy, based as it was on a Ptolemaic world, was a magnificient tribute to his genius. It had but a single flaw. It was wrong!"

ARISTOTLE

Review Questions

1. What was Aristotle's relationship to Alexander the Great?
2. Plato's school was known as the Academy. What was the name of the school founded by Aristotle?
3. Why did Aristotle leave Athens?
4. What is the basic difference between Plato's and Aristotle's views on the nature of man?
5. Name and give an example of each of Aristotle's four causes.
6. In which kind of virtue does man's perfection lie, according to Aristotle? Moral or intellectual?
7. Distinguish and give examples of those virtues which are the same for men and those which differ among them and are relative to each.
8. Up to the Middle Ages, whose thought was more influential on the Christian, Western world? Aristotle's or Plato's?
9. Basically are the following the same or different beings: pure act, prime unmoved mover, self-thinking thought, supreme being?
10. What does the hylemorphic theory mean?

Special Thought Question

Were Aristotle alive today, which kind of government would he favor?

BIBLIOGRAPHY

Primary Source: *Nicomachean Ethics.* Tr. M. Ostwald (New York: Liberal Arts Press, 1962). (Basic ethical teaching of Aristotle.)

Secondary Source: *Aristotle.* Henry Veatch. (Bloomington: Indiana University Press, 1974). (Clearly written overview by a distinguished teacher.)

TRANSITION:

THE FOURTH CENTURY, B.C.
TO THE FOURTH CENTURY, A.D.

Toward the end of the fourth century, B.C., both Greece and philosophy went into decline. With few exceptions, second rate thinkers and followers tried to carry on the work of Socrates, Plato, and Aristotle. An attempt to synthesize, if not compromise, was made by a variety of savants and philosophical schools of thought. They were not blessed with success.

Some, following Socrates, misapplied his teaching on virtue to the point of utter disdain for the sensory side of man. These were the Stoics who have given us the legacy of the adjective, "stoic." It signified one who ignores or holds in contempt any sensory or emotional want.

Others, following Plato, took the path of mysticism, explaining knowledge by intuition and ecstatic contact with a supreme being. Plotinus and the Neo-Platonists of the early Christian era went this route.

Those devoted to Aristotle moved toward excess in becoming pure naturalists and empiricists, ignoring the governing metaphysical bent of their master.

With such "disciples," who need enemies? No wonder it was that a strong trend toward scepticism entered the scene, a fitting tribute to a corrupting culture.

From corruption comes generation, however, and the glory of Rome is in the offing. Philosophically, its strength lay in the area of law, rules of conduct and the practical sphere of life. One thinks of the better elements of Stoicism with the freed slave, Epictetus and the noble emperor, Marcus Aurelius. The genius of an eclectic Cicero also burst upon the scene.

However, challenging the glory of Rome with her own special kind of glory was the phenomenon of Christianity. A religion, rather than a

27

philosophy or ideology, it nonetheless won converts from the highest intellectual circles. A few outstanding examples are Tertullian, Justin and Clement of Alexandria.

Christianity's rapid growth and movement west and north no longer permitted it the luxury of ignoring the wealth of the classical culture of Greece and Rome. In the inevitable confrontation, both were to influence each other, but it was Christianity which was to prevail. The reasons for its success are many and varied, but one was its ability to have outstanding spokesmen and leaders. St. Paul and St. Peter were such men in the first century. In the fourth, one was the great St. Augustine.

4
SAINT AUGUSTINE
(354–430 A.D.)

"I err, therefore, I am." On The Trinity

Faith Seeking Understanding

If we take some liberty with the term, we may place St. Augustine in the lineage of the great existentialists—from Job of the Old Testament to Soren Kierkegaard of nineteenth century Denmark. Like the existentialists, Augustine's philosophy comes to us out of his life experiences and he expresses this philosophy through the media of autobiographical literature. Not that St. Augustine was a philosopher only or even primarily. Theologian and defender of the Faith, he was first and foremost a Christian thinker, wending his way from the city of man to the City of God. His thought is not so much purely philosophical nor even purely theological. Rather it embodied the life long quest for Christian Wisdom.

The Pre-Christian Augustine

Possibly of black lineage, Augustine was born in Tagaste, North Africa in 354 A.D., a time of great moment. His entire life span was caught up in the ongoing merger of the Greco-Roman and the Judeo-Christian traditions. His father was a pagan, but his mother was St. Monica, who lit the spark of faith in the young Augustine. Yet the spark of faith was not to burn brightly for some years to come, for to put it politely, the young Augustine led a rather "full" life.

He studied at Carthage and, indeed, was later to teach Rhetoric, both in Africa and in Rome. Unfortunately, Augustine's experiences as a teacher were rather unhappy. He left Africa because of the rowdiness of his pupils. He fared little better in Rome, when after nearly completing a

29

course under him, Augustine's students left without paying their tuition. (After such experiences, one would have expected Augustine, instead of Boethius, to write a *Consolations of Philosophy.*)

Augustine had always been interested in Christianity, but found the Bible to be somewhat coarse and difficult to interpret. This was due in part to his own aesthetic preferences for the highly polished Latin of the classical writers such as Cicero. It almost was the kind of difference one comes across in reading Chaucer or Shakespeare as opposed to a current newspaper. It was also difficult for his theoretical interest in Christianity to take practical form and govern his lifestyles, for Augustine was a man of great emotion as well as intellect and found it difficult to check his passions. His prayer was always, "Convert me Lord—but not yet!"

In Africa, Augustine kept a mistress for some time and had an illegitimate son whom he named Adeodatus, which means "given by God." Augustine loved his son deeply, and wrote for him. It was a cruel blow to his father when Adeodatus died, still a youth.

Later, in Rome, Augustine took up with another mistress. By this time his mother was ready to disown him, but she talked over her problem with St. Ambrose, the then famous bishop of Milan. He told her that surely God could not refuse to answer the prayers of a woman who was so earnest and preservering. She brought her son to hear the sermons of St. Ambrose and influenced by their depth of ideas and beauty of expression, Augustine grew more favorable to his mother's religion.

Augustine the Convert

Besides the passions of his early manhood, which even include a hint of homosexuality, there probably were two stumbling blocks preventing Augustine's acceptance of his mother's religion. One was his inability to account for evil in the universe of a supposedly all good God; the other was the difficulty of grasping the meaning of spirituality. The first obstacle was one reason why he belonged to the Manichaeans for nine years, a sect which taught that there are two absolute principles—one good and one evil—which govern the universe. This was an offshoot of Persian Zoroastrianism, and although eventually rejected by Augustine, continued to show its influence on his thought until he died. It was carried on in his writings which were transmitted to the high Medieval period—indeed to our own day in both Catholic and Protestant thought.

The second problem was probably one reason why he was inclined to accept scepticism for some time, the view that we cannot know anything for certain.

Eventually, Augustine became enamoured with the philosophy of

Plato as reinterpreted by some of Augustine's contemporaries and predecessors, especially a man called Plotinus, who combined in a spiritual idealism and mysticism, certain notions from philosophy and Christian doctrine. This, together with the sermons of St. Ambrose, helped St. Augustine to see his way through the problem of evil and to get beyond materialism. He came to appreciate that evil was not a positive reality but rather the *lack* of a good that should be present. Blindness, for example, is an evil for man because he lacks the good of vision which should be his. On the other hand, the *absence* of vision in a tree is no evil because it is not proper for a tree to be able to see.

But differently, another example of a physical evil is a dental cary (cavity) in a tooth. What is the cavity? It is not something, but only the lack of something and could and should be present, i.e., the enamel which has been eaten away. It becomes clear that if the cavity takes over the entire tooth, the tooth itself disappears and with it *voila*, the cavity! No tooth, no cavity! This is something like the hole in a doughnut which disappears in the consumption of the doughnut. Evil then is like a parasite; it feeds off the good as long as there is good left from which to feed. When the good ceases to be, evil ceases to be. Hence, one can have good without evil. Accordingly, there can be an all good God, but never an all evil being, for such a being, insofar as it exists, would have some perfection, power or good about it. Augustine now has God "off the hook," for it is evident that there can be evil, but not a God of evil as in Manichaenism, and despite evil, there can be an all good God. A greater understanding of the nature of spirituality now came to Augustine by looking within himself, to the "inner man" rather by looking to things in the world. So it was that Augustine became intellectually, psychologically and spiritually prepared to accept the grace of conversion. It was in a garden in Milan that he heard a child's voice cry out, "Take and read!" With this, he opened an available Bible at random to read a passage in St. Paul which seemed to have especial reference to him, (this practice, stichomanchy, now is condemned). It was not long afterwards that Augustine was baptized into the church. He became a priest, set up a monastic community at Hippo in North Africa and eventually became Bishop of that city. As the Vandals were besieging Hippo, the Goths having sacked Rome earlier, Augustine died in 430.

Augustine the Writer

To appreciate the genius which was Augustine's, one has only to read some of his works. There, the beauty of style, the intensity of emotional experience, the clarity of intellectual insight and the great faith which was his, show forth in all their splendor.

Pick up his *Confessions*, for example. There is the open autobiography and diary of a great tortured soul yearning for the truth, yet struggling so hard against it. There he acknowledges those who have helped fashion his style of life and of thought, for well and for ill. He details the quest for truth which he eventually finds in the opposite place that he had been looking. Truth is not to be found without, but within oneself. "I can find it within, even when I err, for to err, it must at least be true that I exist. (*Si fallor, sum.*)"

This same idea is to be rediscovered over a milennium later by Descartes, when he intuits his famous "Cogito, ergo sum,"—I think hence I am. All in all, *The Confessions* reveal the man, a repentant man who wishes to make a clean breast of everything.

Read his *Soliloquies*, for they reveal Augustine the poet. Sit down with his book, *The Trinity*. It marks him as one of the great theologians. But above all, study his classic, *The City of God*.

The City of God is really a theology of history. By this is meant that for Augustine, history is not cyclical such as experienced by the Greeks and the East in the "myth of eternal return." History is linear and purposive, obeying the orientation given it by the Creator. In this theology of history, Augustine describes two cities, the City of God, heaven, which the Christian seeks as his true home, and the city of man, where we presently reside. In this life, the religious man is only a sojourner passing through earthly existence in order to win eternal salvation. Poetically, one might see these two contrasted as Babylon (the city of man) and the new Jerusalem (the City of God).

Self-love and pleasure provide the shaky foundations of the city of man, but love of God characterizes the pinions of the heavenly city. Still, the city of man can partake of the City of God, if man does not seek Babylon as his end, but places it in proper perspective as a means to man's end, the City of God. At all times we must take to heart St. Paul's reminder, "Though we are in the world, we are not of the world." If we truly love God, that perspective will be won and we may then, "do as we please." Of course, in loving someone, it is what pleases him that pleases us. The lover's pleasure is in abiding the wishes of the beloved. This theme abounds in Augustine and is echoed again in his declaration, "Our hearts are not free, unless they are bound to thee, O Lord."

Truth from Within

Like Plato, Augustine understood man's body as a prison for the spiritual soul. (As one scholar put it, those who despise the body, either do so because they have led too "full" a life, or one which has not been full enough.) To some extent, Augustine, the pleasure seeker now reformed, sought to reform all others. His rather puritanical teachings on human sexuality set a tone for Christianity which only now is being challenged. (It is no accident that the reformer, Augustine, was well hailed in the later Reformation led by Luther and Calvin.)

Yet the lowliness of the body is more due to man's sinfulness, than to his natural condition. The soul, accordingly, is the element in man that should be cultivated. Only it has contact with and participation in the eternal, for it knows truth which is eternal. For example, I know that two plus two equals four and that it forever will be so. Others also know this, so it is a "shared" truth, or, as Plato would say, one in which I participate. Thus since others partake of this same truth, it cannot be from myself (although I am touched by it) but resides preeminently in an eternal being, God. This also is how Augustine interprets Biblical statements such as "I am the Light the cometh into the world," and "I am the Way, the Truth and the Light."

For man, then, truth is to be found in the interior life. Reflection on this interior life reveals that I touch the truth but am not its source. I know this, for I am finite, and changing, while truth is eternal. The source is God, who is synonymous with truth. He resides in me through the truths I know and is both their and my "Inner Master." Whenever I touch upon truth (more properly, when truth touches me), it is by virtue of an inner light of "divine illumination" that God gives me. This enables me to participate in God's eternal ideas.

We can now see how Augustine, while using Plato, altered the Greek's thought to suit Christian purposes. Plato's world of ideas is no longer separated from the One or the Good; for Augustine, these areas are squarely placed in the very mind of God, the creator of all. They serve as blueprints according to which things in the world are made, and so mirror their Creator. We can see how Augustine's thought provides a tighter unity and system by incorporating philosophical notions under the umbrella of theology and religion.

Some of these ideas are innate, but still require an "illumination" to be grasped. Although this is an exaggeration, our mind is like a totally dark room full of furniture which can't be seen until the light is turned on. When the room (mind) is illuminated, we then can see what is present. This latent character of ideas parallels that latent character of things in nature. An acorn, for example latently contains the oak tree. Referring to the order of nature, Augustine gives us a theory of "seminal reasons," a doctrine of physical illumination, which generously interpreted, might look a bit like a theory of evolution.

Augustine now seizes upon the sign of truth present in man's soul as an argument for immortality. Since the soul contains a vestige of immutable and eternal truth, it, too, must have the character of immutability and eternality. It, too, must be immortal. Then again, we can look into our soul and see there the three powers of memory, will and understanding. Numerologist and symbolic thinker that he was, Augustine understood these three powers as a mirror of the Trinity, a kind of reconfirmation of the soul's immortal touch with eternity.

Augustine's Legacy of Problems

As already indicated, Augustine claimed that among various characteristics of God, the two most distinguishing ones were God's unchangeability (immutability) and his eternality (timelessness). Accordingly, things were more godlike and good to the extent that they came closer to being timeless and unchanging. Number and mathematical truths shared this proximity to godlike characteristics. However, the world and especially matter itself reflected this least of all. In this sense, matter was "almost evil," since it always was changing and its grossness farthest removed from imitating God's spirituality. We see in this a hearkening back to Manichaen teachings. Since it is the material things of the world that give pleasure and tempt us from our spiritual path, matter and the things of the world become the source of evil.

Additionally, Augustine was faced with the theological problem of how Original Sin (committed by Adam and Eve) could be transmitted from generation to generation, requiring Baptism of all who would go to heaven. He proposed as a possible solution the notion of Traducianism, the view that somehow this sin was transmitted through the semen in sexual intercourse. It is through such intercourse that Original sin comes to the world. Indeed, Augustine, who for over a decade lived the wild life of a sexual profligate, now came to believe, that intercourse must be tightly restricted. We can see a classic guilt complex coming to be shaped. Indeed, any time pleasure was derived from intercourse, sin was involved. It was only from bare necessity—to propagate the species—that this could be permitted. Intercourse during the menses was strictly prohibited (since procreation could not be forthcoming and the act was taken for pleasure only). Birth control in its various forms including rhythm was roundly condemned. At best, Augustine the reformer, could hold only that intercourse was a necessary evil, and to be avoided as much as possible, yet taking care to serve its purpose of procreation. The position was based on bad physiology (the ancient view was that little "men" swam in the semen and so to "spill one's seed" was virtually equivalent to murder). Recent scholarship also shows it was bad theology. Yet despite this, Augustine's views, which continue to influence Catholic church officials, are almost taken as the norm rather than an aberration.

A further thorny issue emanates from St. Augustine's thought and has yet to be satisfactorily resolved. That is the issue of human freedom and predestination. Augustine firmly holds that God knows from eternity who will be saved and who will be damned. Nothing can alter that judgement. A cursory appraisal of this seems to rule out human freedom. The dilemma involved is that to deny God's foreknowledge of election or damnation seems to take away from his omniscience, his knowing of all things. Yet to admit his omniscience seems to take away human freedom and makes it appear that whatever man does will be of no use. Whom God has chosen, he has chosen! This came to be a major source of conflict in later Protestantism, especially as formulated by John Calvin.

Lastly, Augustine presupposes that immutability is the paradigm of perfection and that our place in the world is that of pilgrims longing to get through this "vale of tears," a world in which all creation "groans and travails." However, in our time of evolutionary theory, immutability seems to be a sign of imperfection. For anything in the world not to change is to cease to be. Change and adaption seem to be perfective elements. This had led some modern theologians to argue not for an unchangeable God, but for one who is in process. Their position is aptly called one of Process Theology. It seems to posit an imperfect God, which others criticize as a contradiction in terms.

The question might also be raised whether we really view ourselves as Pilgrims. In the world of long ago, with sickness prevalent everywhere, often it was a blessing to die. Those who toiled from dawn to dusk doing backbreaking and bone wearying labor, could well have it said when they died, "May they rest in peace!" There are few such parallels in the developed world today, and most feel, if the City of God awaits them, they don't mind waiting a bit longer. Life here isn't that bad. In short, this world more and more is understood as a dwelling place, not a rite of passage and man in a very real sense is viewed as belonging to the earth, no longer apart from, but a part of the earth.

An Appraisal

The writings of St. Augustine are difficult to segment and present piece by piece. To do so would be similar to taking a beautiful statue apart to examine it. Augustine's thought can only be seen as a whole. His entire being is oriented toward bringing the soul out of the city of man to the City of God. Faith, and faith alone, is the light which enables man to grasp the world in its true reality. Yet the faith of which Augustine speaks, is not a blind one but a faith which seeks to understand and to be understood. This theme of a faith *seeking understanding*, of believing, in order to understand, sets the mood for the next 900 years. It is the capital providing the interest to the time of St. Thomas Aquinas in the thirteenth century.

Although it is a great oversimplification, Augustine is the man who Christianized Plato and Platonic philosophy. He is the man who provides the first great synthesis of philosophy and theology in the history of the Church. This synthesis was to continue and undergo further development in the next 1,000 years, yet, in the opinion of many, it had a mortal shortcoming—a weakness which was to be fully exploited by St. Thomas Aquinas.

What was that shortcoming? Basically, it was that the philosophical ideas which Augustine wedded to his Christian theology, never quite fit their religious counterpart. Augustine's philosophy was largely drawn from Plato and interpreters of Plato. Now Plato's philosophy was a system of essences, whereas Augustine's theology was one of Christian life and existence. While the two systems may have made a great friendship, they never should have been married by Augustine who performed the hasty ceremony. And yet we must be fair and understand that although Augustine used Platonic expressions, he did not necessarily commit himself to all of their deep implications. Rather, they were a way of getting off "dead center," of getting started in his system and then going his own way. It is a path many have travelled.

ST. AUGUSTINE

Review Questions

1. Show how the times and culture of Augustine affect his own life which can be divided into the two stages of before and after his conversion to Christianity.
2. What were the two major intellectual problems which blocked and delayed Augustine's conversion?
3. Who were the Manichaeans and what was their influence on Augustine?
4. Name two persons who were positive influences on Augustine.
5. What is the name of Augustine's most autobiographical work?
6. For Augustine, what is the proper relationship between man and the world in which man presently lives?
7. Is Augustine closer to Plato or Aristotle in thought and in what ways?
8. Who is the Inner Master and how does one attain truth?
9. What is meant by the Augustinian theme, "faith seeking understanding?"
10. Although Augustine lived for a time in Italy, he was born, served as Bishop and died in the northern part of what continent?

Special Thought Question

In what ways has Augustine exerted major influence on Christianity, for good and for ill?

BIBLIOGRAPHY

Primary Source: *The Essential Augustine.* Ed. Vernon J. Bourke (New York: The New American Library, 1964). (Selection of parts of Augustine's various writings.)

Secondary Source: *Saint Augustine.* Henri Marrou. Tr. by Patrick Hepburne-Scott (New York: Harper Torchbooks, 1957). (Covers the life, doctrines and influence of Augustine.)

TRANSITION:

THE FIFTH TO THE THIRTEENTH CENTURY

Augustine died in 430 as the Vandals were laying siege to Hippo. Earlier in 410, Rome had been sacked by the barbarians, an event that signaled the collapse of the glory of Rome. For the next five centuries, the West spent the greater part of its energies in preserving what heritage was left, transmitting that heritage to future generations and gradually building up a momentum that would break forth in the High Middle Ages. Little original thought developed during this period. Boethius (480–525) did write his famous *Consolations of Philosophy* and translated some of the works of Aristotle (especially parts of the *Logic*), but except for such isolated instances of progress, the status quo prevailed. By way of a "holding action" only, learning was preserved in the monasteries where books were also copied and reproduced.

With Charlemagne (742–814), a famous Palatine School was set up, and great teacher-scholars were imported to serve as Masters. Three such outstanding men were Alcuin, Rhabanus Maurus and John Scotus Eriugena. Eventually cathedral schools were founded and these, in turn, were to serve as the base for the great universities to follow.

The dark period of the Middle Ages is beginning to dissipate and with St. Anselm (1033–1109) we find the beginnings of the philosophical-theological era of scholasticism. This period is marked as scholastic by its rather pedantic mode of argumentation, its style of writing various summaries, commentaries, and disputed questions, and by its deductivistic (but not rationalist) methodology. The great thinkers in the Latin West at this time were generally clergy and religious. They shared a common language of Latin and a common Christian culture. For most, philosophy was a handmaid to theology, but not an abused slave of it. Despite the common features, however, this was a time of great controversy; marked by outstanding intellectual ferment.

Anselm's own thought is characterized as original, yet in continuity with the spirit of St. Augustine, exemplified by a "faith seeking to be understood." He is well known in philosophy for his famous "ontological proof" for the existence of God. It is an attempt to see within the concept of God in man's mind the necessity for the existence of God outside of man's mind.

After Anselm, emphasis was given to logic, as was to be expected, for it was the logic of Aristotle that first reached the Middle Ages, rather than his more profound metaphysical treatises. As a consequence, the "problem of universals" was a major issue at the time. This problem concerns whether or not the general nature of things expressed in concepts, exists in that manner in the real world. Abelard (1079–1142) figured prominently in this controversy.

With the exceptions noted then (and a few others) the Latin West did not produce great philosophers in the early part of the Middle Ages. However, the Arab world did generate magnificent thinkers. This world reached its apex in the eleventh and twelfth centuries. In the East, the dominant figure was Avicenna (980–1036). Born in Persia, a physician, philosopher and man of genius, Avicenna took advantage of the works of Aristotle available to the Arab world, but as yet unknown or inaccessible to the Latin West. Also influenced by Neo-Platonism, his philosophy represents a synthesis of Greek science and philosophy with Islamic overtones. His importance can scarcely be underestimated and St. Thomas later is to draw heavily upon his ideas.

As the Arab empire coursed westward and even into Spain, we come upon another outstanding thinker, Averroes (1126–1198). For Averroes, Aristotle was always *the* philosopher, and Averroes wrote long and detailed commentaries on Aristotle's works. For that reason, St. Thomas was to favor Averroes with the description, "The Commentator." Averroes held that human reason is supreme. Accordingly, biblical stories of miracles, etc., are to be interpreted only allegorically. This met the strong objection of Arab theologians and they battled Averroes aggressively. The Arabian genius for science, especially mathematics and astronomy, coupled with a messianic and militaristic religious fervor was bound to clash. Clearly, the problem of faith and reason was a central one for Arab and Christian alike.

Before we move to the higher Middle Ages, one additional contribution to the tenor of the times must be noted. That is the legacy of two brilliant Jewish thinkers. The first is Avicebron (c. 1021–1070) who wrote in Arabic and who authored the widely read book known to the Latins as *Fount of Life*. Even more important however was Rabbi Moses

Maimonides (1135–1204). A gifted philosopher and theologian, living in Spain, he attempted to reconcile Aristotle with Judaism, where such ameliorization was thought possible. Also an influence on St. Thomas, his *Guide for the Perplexed* is a classic summation of Jewish theology.

Back in the Latin West, thinkers were coming increasingly into contact with the whole corpus of Aristotle's writings as well as with the wealth of Moslem culture. The contact with the Arabs in Spain and the various Crusades opened up this rich and formidable avenue of learning. Couple this with the founding of the two great mendicant orders of Franciscans (1214) and Dominicans (1217) and the growth of the universities and one finds that the thirteenth century is one of immense interest, controversy, and intellectual and religious stimulation.

In Toledo and Seville and in Sicily at the court of Frederick II, great translators worked to make intelligible the new sources of learning for those who could not read the original documents. Oxford excelled in the study of science, Montpelier in medicine, and Bologna in law. But the best known and most controversial international university was Paris where theology was its forte. Popes were numbered among its alumni and the university was regarded as a bellwether and watched closely for trends—and heresies. St. Albert, St. Bonaventure and St. Thomas are among its many famous Masters.

It is the thought of the latter, Thomas Aquinas, that we will now examine, for he represents the highest genius of this period of gifted intellectuals. In the Roman Catholic Church, his synthesis of faith and reason became guidelines for philosophical patterns enduring for seven centuries.

5

SAINT THOMAS AQUINAS (1224/5–1274)

"Reason in man is rather like God in the world."
On Kingship

Light of the Dark Ages

The thirteenth century is often thought of as the Dark Ages. In some respects, it was a dark and barbarian age, but in others it was an age of immense controversy and light. It was an age in which the great universities of western civilization were getting started—the universities of Paris, Oxford, Cambridge, Toulouse, Naples, etc. It was an age which saw the birth of two great orders of the Church, the Dominicans and the Franciscans. It was an age in which the tremendous force of Greek and Arabic culture coming into the West forced the West to make a thorough going over and often agonizing reappraisal of science, philosophy, faith and reason. It was the century that witnessed the birth of a boy baby from the Diocese of Aquino, near Naples, Italy. He came into the world in 1224/5. His family called him by his Christian name of Tomaso. For seven centuries since, the entire West knew him as St. Thomas Aquinas, the greatest of the doctors of the Church.

Beggerman or Chief?

St. Thomas was born into a family with royal blood and he knew personally many of the rulers and Popes of the age. He received a wonderful education at such places as the famed Benedictine monastery, Monte Cassino (which still stands to this day), the University of Naples, Cologne and the University of Paris. It is quite possible that his parents had high hopes for his attaining a position of power and perhaps some degree of wealth, for they objected strenuously when he joined the newly formed mendicant order of Dominicans.

His parents had no quarrel with Thomas becoming a priest, for after all, popes and cardinals were priests and had their share of wealth and power. But a mendicant—one who took vows of poverty—that was different!

However, Thomas' will prevailed and he eventually found himself studying under such masters as Albert the Great. Thomas graduated from the most cosmopolitan of the medieval universities, Paris, in 1256. He was awarded the Magister's degree, slightly above our doctorate. But even this was not without incident.

Center of Controversy

It seems that the secular or regular clergy were unhappy with the new mendicant orders getting university educations and then seeking teaching positions in the university system. Because of this "closed shop" attitude, the university refused to grant the degrees earned by St. Thomas (and by his friend, the Franciscan, St. Bonaventure) until a Papal Bull ordered the authorities to do so.

There is something symbolic in this controversy, for throughout his life Aquinas was to stand squarely in the middle of countless storms, political, academic and religious. His own family had been caught up in a dual allegiance to the warring papacy and various monarchs. Indeed, one of his brothers was executed for treason.

Within the university, Thomas withstood strikes and boycotts and he even preached under police protection, he defended himself against charges of defamation of character and of heresy. Such attacks came from without *and* within his own Religious Order. In all of these battles, Aquinas stood his ground, almost serenely and treated his opponents with great respect, but the truth, with greater respect. Thomas Aquinas died at about 50 years of age in 1274, but his wisdom and sanctity came to be known and appreciated more and more, not only in the Church, but throughout the world.

Because of his great interest and writings on angels, he was called the "Angelic Doctor" by the Church. Popes throughout the ages have paid him homage and his system of theology came to be particularly favored by the Roman Catholic Church, which felt that no one studying Thomas could stray far from the truth. He was canonized a saint in 1323, his early teacher, Albert, not winning that recognition until the twentieth century.

To win a better appreciation of the odds which Thomas was up against in shifting the intellectual horizons of the Church and in reality, the entire Latin West, it will be helpful to sketch further the background of his times.

Aristotle Replaces Plato in the West

Picture in an age dominated by authority, the great authority of St. Augustine which had lorded over the philosophical and theological science in the Church for about 800 years. It was and remains a great theology, but its philosophical heritage, to use St. Thomas's expression, was "imbued" with Platonic philosophy. Now along comes a young upstart who wishes to replace many of the Platonic underpinnings with a philosophy based on the pagan, Aristotle. Such an idea was nothing short of scandalous to the age, but sometimes, scandal must prevail, and prevail it did.

St. Thomas' success, in large measure, was due to the intrinsic merits of his views; in small measure, it was due to his ability to render a "reverential interpretation" to the writings of his predecessors. Instead of coming out directly and saying, this or that man was dead wrong, he would reinterpret the writings to a view more favorable to his own. Thus, from all appearances, he would gather many opponents to his own side. (It is claimed that St. Thomas would have been highly successful in the diplomatic corps had he missed his original calling, for in fact, many of the interpretations he attributed to others would make them turn over in their graves. It was like stating, "Yes, that is what Augustine said, but this is what he meant!")

Although St. Thomas was of Aristotelian lineage in philosophy, he took truth wherever it could be found. If this meant rejecting Aristotle on some counts, Thomas had no hesitancy in doing so. If it meant gathering some insights from Jewish or Arabian thinkers, he went straight to them and acknowledged his indebtedness. His most original contribution is the role "existence" plays in his philosophy.

The God Problem

The problem as to whether or not we can know God in a sort of positive way is resolved by a kind of philosophical compromise. The issue is not as some have misput it, how can a finite being bridge the gap to knowing an infinite being. After all, if God is a cause of creatures, that is, if we are his effects, then by studying the effects we can come to know something about the cause, at least that it exists. And we know creatures are effects from several observations, one of which is the fact that creatures come into being—that their being is not from themselves but from something else. This leads to the notion of an ultimate being, whose existence is not

43

from another, but who has it in his own right—*ipsum esse.*

Aquinas indicates then that through reasoning based on experience, we can truly know that there is a God—that He is good, providential, infinite and so on. Yet, St. Thomas also points out that this knowledge is very inadequate, that in fact, we know more what God is not, than what He is! Yet the important thing is that we can know some thing about God, even without the aid of religion. In fact, using Aristotle, he proves that the goal of all men is to know God. The argument in skeletal form is this: The end of man must lie in a perfection of his highest power. Now the highest power of man is clearly the intellect. Thus, the end of man must consist primarily in an intellectual activity.

Now, as an object of knowledge, what is most intelligible, most understandable? Strictly speaking, God is the most intelligible of all things. He then, is the being whose intelligibility we will never fully exhaust, hence, knowing God is primarily the end of man.

There are other pointers to God also. For example, order in the world, changes of the seasons, planetary movements, laws of nature, etc., all demand an intelligent orderer. Then too the fact that we observe causes in the world, whose causality is not from themselves absolutely, but are *caused causes* as it were. To illustrate, in writing on the blackboard, the chalk is a genuine cause to the writing, but always and only under the direction of a higher cause, in this case the teacher. The chalk then is a caused cause. By following up on a series of caused causes, we eventually are led to an *uncaused cause*, namely God. There also is the argument from *consensus universalis*, which says that in some way, often admittedly vague, nearly everyone has from all time believed in some sort of a supreme being. In a way, for Aquinas, all men know God, but they do not always know it is God they know. For example, if I see a man in the distance (who happens to be my friend, although I don't know this at the distance that it is my friend), I see my friend but do not know it is my friend whom I see. When we look at beauty in nature, etc. it is God we see but often we are not aware of this.

Now our knowledge about God through philosophy is indirect, at best. That is, we can know of God and his powers or attributes only by *analogy.* By this is meant that anything we can say of God from our knowledge of the world has a meaning that is not exactly, but only partly the same and different. For example, the relationship of an apprentice to a journeyman in the trades, is analogous to the relationship of a graduate assistant to a Professor. There is a certain likeness there, a certain proportionality. Thus we can truly declare God is Good (method of *attribution,* predicating of God perfections found in creatures), but he is not good in exactly the same way as creatures are good (method of negation or *removal,* which denies any imperfections that may accompany creatural goodness). Lastly we may say that he is good in the highest possible manner (method of *excellence*). To sum up, nothing can be said exactly of God in the way it can be said of creatures (univocal use of terms), but neither is everything that is said of God, purely misleading (equivocal use of terms), but things can be said of God with some limited meaning (analogous use of terms). All in all we can readily see what is called the "God—problem" really is the problem of man!

Although he agrees with Augustine that God is eternal and unchangeable, these are not God's primary attributes for Aquinas. The chief earmark of God and his greatest mark of distinction is that in God, essence and existence are identical. This means that God is pure perfection, that there is none prior, that He cannot not exist. In short, Augustine put the cart before the horse. It is because God is a necessary existence, that He is eternal and unchangeable, not the other way around. Creatures have their existence from another, God has his existence of himself. God is *ipsum esse*.

Qualifiers of the Human Condition

Given the limited condition of man, and despite Aquinas's view that the highest end of man (*summum bonum*) consists in knowing God, Aquinas qualifies his position. In the present life, we can love more than we can know—whether it be a lofty being such as God or our next door neighbor. Hence, here on earth it is better to love God than to know him. Happily this love is accessible to all, while high level philosophy that produces knowledge is available only to the few.

In a certain way, such love can even produce a kind of knowledge of its own. Love can exceed knowledge, given our present situation, because love proceeds from the will, while knowing proceeds from intellect. Now all knowing (residing in the knower) is in a certain way on the same level, namely, the level of the knower. If we know something lower than ourselves, we bring it up to our level to understand it. An example is the material world which we abstract in order to know it intellectually. The material world exists as matter, but we dematerialize it and lift it to an abstract and immaterial level commensurate with our intellect. Similarly, to know what is above us, for example, God, we must bring Him down to our level to grasp Him. And for this reason, we tend to picture God like his creatures which we do know directly.

Will (and accordingly, love which proceeds from it), unlike intellect, however, always seeks the object it loves in itself, as it is in the real order. For example, a picture of an ice cream cone in a little boy's imagination on a hot summer day is no consolation to him. What he desires is the real ice cream cone in the real order. Love, then, does not stay at the level of the lover, but goes to the real existence of the beloved. That is why, when we love something lower than our own dignity, in a sense, we lower and debase ourselves; whereas if we love something which is lofty and above ourselves, such as God, we more or less "pull ourselves up by our own bootstraps" to that object. The lover then "goes out" of himself; the knower brings things "into" himself. In a limited sense, Aquinas thus comes back to Augustine's famous, "Love . . . and do as you please."

Faith and Reason

Another of the vexing problems with which the great thinkers of St. Thomas' age were faced, was the problem of the relationship of faith and reason. Did faith contradict reason? Could one be true and the other false? Could faith and reason both oppose each other and both still be true? There are many answers given to this by those who applied themselves to the problem.

The great Jewish philosopher, Moses Maimonides (whom St. Thomas affectionately called Rabbi Moses) struggled with this problem and tried to reconcile the teachings of Aristotle with those of the Jewish faith. The great Arabian philosophers, Avicenna (who was actually from Persia) and Averroes (who hailed from Spain) also applied themselves to this problem. The position of Averroes was that when there was a conflict between faith and reason, it would be faith which had to go. Some say he even gave rise to the position that both could oppose each other and both yet be true, each in its own way. This interpretation has it that faith and sacred writings are allegorical, written for those who are not bright enough to use reason which sees the truth directly.

St. Thomas begins his position with the principle that truth is one. Nothing in reason could ever contradict faith. On the other hand, nothing in faith could contradict reason. If one is right, the other, if it contradicts it, is wrong. St. Thomas pointed out that some things known by faith could be demonstrated by reason. Thomas terms these the *preambles of faith*. For example, the existence of God, the immortality of the human soul, the fact that there is only one God, etc. Now, of course, there are some people, who because of a lack of background and perhaps native intelligence, who could not grasp the proofs for these. Such could accept these truths from Faith, while others could see them to be true by reason and experience.

On the other hand, some of the truths of Faith are so far above man, that he could never hope to demonstrate or prove them. Such would be the dogma that there are three persons in one God. These are termed *articles of faith*. To attempt to prove these by reason, would only make onself and one's Faith appear ridiculous to an unbeliever. These things,

Aquinas showed, we accept on Faith. Yet, negatively, even here we can show that there is no contradiction in the doctrines of faith. It is not that these truths are unintelligible, it is that they are too intelligible for our human condition. The light of such truths is so brilliant that it blinds us.

Similar to Augustine, St. Thomas takes up the problem of predestination and free will, but again the solution to this problem is equally unsatisfactory. I believe St. Thomas would admit this himself, eventually declaring it a mystery and not fully penetrable by man. He does shed some light on it however by posing the following clarification. Let us see if we can follow his thought.

If I see that you are reading, it is *necessary* that you are reading (else how could I see that you are doing that?). Yet my seeing you read, *does not impose any necessity* on your reading, for at any time you can put down the book and do something else. If God sees that we will be saved, we will be saved (or damned, as the case might be), but this *does not impose any necessity* on one's being saved or damned. Put another way, if God foresees that I will act freely, then it is necessary that I act freely! Again there is no imposition of necessity by God just because he sees me acting freely. But now comes the hitch! How can God know which way my will, will act, which way it will choose? Aquinas suggests it is because God wills it from eternity and at the proper moment in time moves man's will to so act and in acting, to choose this or that act. The plot thickens! How then can man be free? St. Thomas answers that only God can move the will to act in accord with its own nature, i.e., to act freely. Thus God's movement on the will, permits and moreso, enables the will to act freely.

Obviously there is something very unsatisfactory in the above and the suggested explanation drew great rebuttals from others in the Church offering their own explanation. Finally, the Pope stepped in and told each of the parties in effect not to call the other heretics. No one really knows how to explain it. Nonetheless, although it offers a different interpretation than does Calvinism, the Catholic Church does hold to a doctrine of predestination.

Man

St. Thomas's views on the nature of man are interesting and represent a sharp departure from some of the Platonic-Augustinian views which then were prevalent. For Thomas, man is not simply an embodied soul, with the body as something unnatural and harmful to the soul. Man is the essential union of soul *and* matter. This is man's natural condition. The soul of man is naturally immortal, but it still retains an exigency for the body, which by faith, we know will be reunited to it. Although it cannot be developed here, the Angelic Doctor's understanding of man as person, rather than simply as individual are remarkable in their implication and application. Person implies a certain wholeness, such that neither body nor soul is a person. Only the unity that results from these is a human person. What this means is that Aquinas does not attempt to argue philosophically for the immortality of the person, for as with Aristotle, he sees that humans die, not just their bodies (Plato). Of course, theologically, Aquinas accepts the restoration of the person at the Day of Judgement.

Philosophy only demonstrates the immortality of man's soul, which is but one of his essential parts. Hence for those who accept the doctrine of Purgatory, according to this no persons are there, only human souls. Those who speak of persons in Purgatory do so from a Platonic/Augustinian perspective, a perspective which confuses soul for person.

Lastly and consistent with his Aristotelian-based views on man, Thomas holds that whatever ideas and knowledge man comes to have, he comes to have through sensory experience as its basis. Man is not born with any preconceived notions or thought. There is not even an inborn idea of God in man. Together with Aristotle, Thomas could say that there is nothing in the intellect which has not first, and in some way, come through the senses.

Law

Another area of St. Thomas' thought which is being restudied today is his discussion of law, especially natural law. This, for Aquinas, is man's "conscious and rational participation in the Eternal Law of God." The Natural Moral Law, then, is not something written on tablets, but something that man, through reason, makes out of his understanding of reality. Law, then, is always on "ordinance of reason." If a law violates the order of reason, strictly speaking, it is no law. In this sense, reason is objective and reality is its standard available to all normal men. The nature of men being basically the same, demands that what is inherently wrong be everywhere so and for all times. On the other hand, many acts which may be wrong but only by virtue of peculiar circumstances, might be permitted and even praiseworthy given a change of conditions.

Interest in natural law theory is on the rise again and Aquinas' views are being reexamined. John Rawl's theory of justice moves in this direction as does the philosophical basis for the United Nations and the legal justification of the Nuremberg trails. There seems to be a continuity in what men think as basically right or basically wrong. There seems to be a common human nature in which we all participate as part of a larger Nature itself. Else, as Walter Lippman, a great political philosopher once asked, "Why do old men plant trees under whose shade they will never sit?".

Thomas' Mature Years

St. Thomas' adult life was spent commuting between Italy, where he taught theology at the papal courts, and Paris, where he taught theology at the University. During this time, he turned out many volumes of writings, among which is the *Summary of Theology*, truly one of his masterpieces. This work alone, contains over 3,000 separate articles of discussion and answers over 10,000 objections to various problems in philosophy and theology. And this is only one of his many, many works! What is especially noteworthy is the consistency of his views from his earliest work, *On Being and Essence* to his last writings in theology.

Besides his scholarly writings, with equal ease and dedication, Thomas taught, composed hymns and prayers and participated in the activities of his religious community.

Thomism Today

For the age in which he lived, St. Thomas' views were revolutionary. So revolutionary, in fact, that many received local condemnations by some of the Bishops of the time! Yet the general synthesis of philosophy and theology by St. Thomas Aquinas has stood the test of time. Not only has it stood this test, but it has been reinforced, so that today, Thomistic philosophy, or Thomism as it is popularly called, has assumed a new vitality. This vitality is seen, not as a closed system (for a true philosophy can never close its doors to reality), but as providing a ready framework in which one can search for truth openly. There can be little doubt that this is as St. Thomas Aquinas, the great "scholastic" of the Middle Ages, would have wished it to be.

ST. THOMAS AQUINAS

Review Questions

1. Describe the changes in the Church and society which gave such momentum to the thirteenth century as the most important in the Middle Ages.
2. Name the university from which St. Thomas graduated and where he taught for many years.
3. Although Aquinas drew heavily from a host of predecessors, the greatest philosophical influence upon him was from what thinker?
4. For St. Thomas, which is better: to love God or to know him? Why and in what respects?
5. Name two who wrote in Arabian and one Jewish thinker who influenced St. Thomas' thought.
6. Is it ever possible for faith to contradict reason or reason to contradict faith? Why or why not?
7. How does St. Thomas' philosophy represent a rather sharp turnaround from the previous nine centuries of Christian thought?
8. How does man acquire knowledge for Aquinas? Does man ever have any innate ideas, such as that of God?
9. What does Aquinas understand by "law?"
10. What is the greatest overall contribution made by Aquinas?

Special Thought Question

If law is an "ordinance of reason," can an unjust law be a law and need it be obeyed?

BIBLIOGRAPHY

Primary Source: Introduction to Saint Thomas Aquinas. Ed. A. C. Pegis (New York: Modern Library, 1948). (A selection of texts from a broad spectrum of Aquinas' writings.)

Secondary Source: Aquinas. F. C. Copleston (Baltimore: Penguin Books, 1955). (Excellent overview of St. Thomas specifically directed to the beginner.)

TRANSITION:

FOURTEENTH TO THE SEVENTEENTH CENTURY

After St. Thomas, the Middle Ages witnessed a general decline from which it was never to recover. Occasionally, bright lights appeared on the horizon but they could not forestall the oncoming rush of a new age, the modern era. Exercising temporary holding action were such men as Dante (1265–1321), the great philosopher-literary genius; the Franciscan, Duns Scotus (1265–1308), and later, Francis Suarez the Jesuit (1548–1617). They represented the last vestiges of philosophical pluralism known to the High Middle Ages. Now, it was no longer individuals, but schools of thought which developed, e.g., Thomism, Scotism, Suarezianism. Such schools often became self-serving, a spirit quite at odds with their masters.

The fourteenth to seventeenth centuries were marked by great social, political and religious troubles. These forged the changing future of philosophy and Europe. This change was furthered by the Renaissance of the fifteenth-sixteenth centuries which gave birth to a new interpretation of humanism. The invention of moveable type by Samuel Gutenberg (1397–1468) also sped the transition. Additionally, the layman was coming into his own and replaced the clergy and religious as movers of men's minds. The entrance of the layman into philosophy saw publication of works no longer exclusively in the language of the Church (Latin), but in the vernacular as well. The layman addressed himself less to apologetics and theological questions, and more to secular and political problems and to science. It was science which was to prosper most for the next six centuries. Although a simplification, science in the Latin Middle Ages was subject to philosophy which in turn served as handmaid to theology, the self-proclaimed Queen of all. In an Age of Faith this was understandable, but in the coming Age of Reason it was intolerable and theology fell into disrepute, while philosophy served its new mistress, science.

The new age emphasized man as citizen of the earth rather than heir to heaven. Erasmus (1466–1536) and Francis Bacon (1561–1626) are but two typical exponents. Bacon, the trumpeteer (rather than practitioner) of the new science summed up the changing attitude with his principle, "Knowledge and power meet in one!" Knowledge was to be sought for the practical benefits it confers upon men. That is why Bacon urged us to imitate bees rather than spiders. Spiders were like the philosophers of old, spinning their rationalistic web out of materials from their own innards. Bees, however, went to work on nature herself and making honey from pollen, transmuted nature's product into one for their own use. The new logic henceforth would be inductive rather than deductive, a logic of discovery, not one of exposition.

So it was that the new era which came to be known as that of Modern Philosophy was an era of discovery; discovery about man, the earth, the society he lived in.

6
RENÉ DESCARTES (1596–1650)

"It is not enough to have a good mind. The main thing is to use it well." Discourse on Method

Father of Modern Philosophy

They are the fading years of the sixteenth century. Great men have just died and great men are being born. For centuries to come, both will shape the worlds of science, mathematics, religion and philosophy. Their names read like a Who's Who: Luther, Calvin, Copernicus, Bacon, Galileo, Gilbert, Keppler, and the list goes on and on. Near the top of this list is a young, Catholic Frenchman, without a knowledge of whom, one cannot understand the movement of philosophy for the next three hundred years. His name was René Descartes.

The Problem with Philosophy

Descartes was born in La Haye, France in 1596 and studied at various centers of learning, acquiring considerable knowledge about law, medicine (body dissection was coming into vogue now), mathematics and philosophy. It was in this last area, namely philosophy, that confusion appeared to be the order of the day. Mathematics was simple enough. Get men to agree on what one means by a straight line, by a triangle and so on, and if one is logical, one can show them certain conclusions deriving from a set of principles. There are conclusions they cannot help but agree on, having previously accepted the basic principles and definitions. As a matter of fact, Descartes obliged the sceptics here, by going so far as to invent what all high schoolers know as analytic geometry.

Now the case obviously was different in philosophy where two things struck the attention of Descartes. Philosophy seemed to have made almost no progress since the days of its Greek beginnings. In addition, it appeared that seldom, if ever, do philosophers agree. Mathematicians and scientists might have their quarrels, but these could be resolved by careful reasoning, observation and experimentation. Once resolved, these disciplines built higher structures on their new solid foundations and in doing so advanced their cause, which is the progress of mankind. Descartes was going to remedy this scandalous lack in philosophy, the lack of progress and the lack of agreement among its interpreters and exponents.

The dream of accomplishing this and the general outlines to be followed came to Descartes when he was serving in the army in Germany around 1619. After Descartes completed his formal education with the Jesuits, he thought he would learn a good deal about the world if he could travel and have the leisure time to study it. Logical man that he was, he joined several armies to accomplish this goal. In those days, armies seldom fought during the winter or on religious holidays, so this respite proved to be a good time for meditating on different problems. Descartes used to curl up inside the old bread ovens or kilns to keep warm. There he would work out his ideas. What he envisaged in a famous dream was his producing a kind of universal mathematics or science and applying this to philosophy. His remaining life, much of it spent in Holland, was oriented toward trying to make that dream come true. As he modestly put it, he wanted "to acquire a certain and clear knowledge of all those things which could be of some use to men for life."

The Indubitable Method

According to Descartes, all that philosophy needed to get off of "dead center" where it had been languishing for centuries, was a good rigorous method at its disposal. Once agreement was won here, everything else would fall into place, philosophy would advance, and philosophers would live happily together ever after. This is pretty much they way Descartes pictured it, for he was an inveterate optimist. The only way we can go wrong, said Descartes, was to deviate from the method. Any intellectual error we make is going to be rooted in the will, because it was not resolute enough to follow the method advocated by Descartes. As one scholar puts it, for Descartes, intellectual error is practically a sin, for error essentially is a result of intellectual carelessness. To understand this, let's look to a game of tic tac toe or perhaps for those more gifted, the game of chess. Whenever one loses, he will give as an excuse that he didn't see the consequences of his bad move. The reason is because he failed to concentrate sufficiently. Now that the move cannot be taken back, he sees his mistake—a lack of foresight caused by impatience at further concentration. To prevent this "sin," Descartes shows us a foolproof plan. It is his book, *Discourse on Method*.

Uncertainty of the Senses

Well, says Descartes, let's start from scratch. Can I be certain of anything at all? The sense world *seems* to exist outside of myself, I *seem* to sense birds, trees, animals and in general what is called the external world. But wait, cautions Descartes! There are some times when my senses deceive me. For example, the color *blue* looks *black* under a certain light, a *straight* stick, if put into water appears to be *bent*, we often see mirages. Hence, it is apparent that sometimes the senses deceive me. Now if they deceive me sometimes, how can I be sure they do not deceive me at other times when I think they are true? I can even apply this to the dreaming and waking periods of life. There are times when I am dreaming and believe myself to be awake. Many of us have had dreams in which (within the dream itself) we ask if we're awake or asleep. We say, "I'll pinch myself to see if I'm awake." We do so and are convinced we are not dreaming. Then an hour later we awake! Can it be that when I now think myself awake, I might be dreaming. If anything is obvious at this point, it is that the senses are not to be trusted, at least as a starting point in the quest for certitude.

Thus, whereas Aristotle began his philosophy in a state of *wonder*, Descartes commences his in a state of *doubt*, albeit methodical doubt, rather than sceptical doubt. In short, Descartes is suspending his judgement about contact with reality, etc. It is not a "real" doubt, but as he says, it is a methodical doubt, a kind of hypothesis posited to see where it might lead. To keep his life in order, he is not going to doubt the political or religious facts of life, but give them provisional acceptance. Not to do so could get him into serious trouble with the State and/or Church. He had an object lesson shown him when he learned of Galileo's difficulties with the Church. Descartes was in full agreement with Galileo, but given the circumstances was prudent not to advertise this.

Certainty of the Self

Yet Descartes is not going to remain in doubt for long, for the doubts that I entertain, says Descartes, are going to give rise to certitude. How, one may ask, is that possible? Quite simple! No matter how much I doubt, I remain convinced of at least one thing, namely, that I am—that I exist! Even if I doubt my existence, this makes my existence certain, for I could not doubt I am, unless I already exist! Cf. the similarity to St. Augustine's statement of "I err, therefore I am."

Descartes is now ready to formulate the first principle of his philosophy and he considers himself to be well on the way now to establishing a universal method. That first truth which he has seen is familiar to us all, *cogito, ergo sum!* I think, hence, I am! This truth is unshakeable, it cannot be doubted, for to doubt at least is to be, to exist! (It is important to clarify that the term "thinking" is used in a most general way. It includes feeling, willing, doubting, etc., in short every state of consciousness.)

Now *to be thinking* are words which might be numbered (1) *to;* (2) *be;* (3) *thinking.* I cannot get to (3) without first having (1) and (2). This is not so much a reasoning process, for it is so elementary that it is in intuition, an insight, that to be thinking is to be.

Descartes' philosophy now has found its bedrock and begins with this idea of the self, the ego, the consciousness. What am I? I am a "thinking thing." This idea of self as a "thinking thing" (which for the moment, does not include my body) is now carefully examined. He sees in this idea, two characteristics which mark it as a true idea, and which henceforth will serve as the marks of all true ideas. Where I find these marks, the idea will be true. They are marks of being *clear* and *distinct.* If I know what an alligator is, my idea is clear. If I can enumerate its differences from those of a crocodile, it also is distinct.

Certainty of God

Now searching my consciousness, I find there another idea present to it. It is an overwhelming idea. It is the idea of God, an idea of a being infinite, all powerful, all good and so on. Yet Descartes is very cautious in accepting this idea. Perhaps it is a fabrication of his own mind. After all, I make up silly non-existent things all the time. I can picture a winged horse such as Pegasus, yet one doesn't actually exist. I can picture a mermaid, or as one wit put it, a maidmer (that's where the top half is a fish). But no, the idea of God is radically different from those others which I invent at will from bits and pieces of my experience, only put together in a new way. The idea of God is of a being more perfect than myself, of a being infinitely perfect. Hence, the idea cannot have come from myself, as if I made it up, or from the external world. After all, how could the perfect come from the imperfect self or world? No, Descartes argued, this innate idea could only come from one source—a being who *is* all perfect, God! This idea of God must also be true then, for it, too, is clear and distinct.

To put it succinctly, God, not myself, is the cause of this infinite idea. Starting with this idea, as an effect that cannot be explained by my own imagination, I must conclude or deduce that someone else put it in my mind. This is its cause, God. This method of argument moves from effect to cause and is rather traditional (although not as Descartes applied it here). This type of reasoning is termed *a posteriori.*

If I desire, I also can look at the very nature of the idea of God rather than for its cause, and prove God that way, too. For example, in under-standing a triangle, I understand at the same time, certain of its properties such as "having angles equal to 180 degrees." In understanding my idea of God, I see in the nature expressed by that idea, that God's essence or nature as a perfect being demands that he really exists. Here was a proof so simple that even the untutored could grasp it. Many in the Church praised Descartes for this contribution to what is known as "the ontologi-cal argument," but others thought it involved a vicious circle. Traditionally, this kind of argument, moving as it does from the nature of a thing to its necessary properties, is termed an *a priori* argument.

Certainty of the World

There yet remains for Descartes, the difficulty of bridging the gap be-tween the *self* and the external *world*. Hence, he now sets out to do something strange, even for philosophers. He seeks to prove the existence of such a material world. (We must remember that up to this point, he has only demonstrated his own existence as a mind and the existence of a spiritual God.) He accomplishes the proof for the reality of matter through utilizing the contents of his concept of God. Since there is a God, and since God is all good, He clearly cannot be a deceiver.

Now my mind keeps making me believe that there is a real and material world. I believe that I have senses and a body that establish contact with such a world. If there isn't such a world, I would be in constant deception. The blame would be placed on God who is my maker, who made me in such a way as to keep deceiving me. But this is impossible, since God is not a deceiver. (It is obvious Descartes has envisioned a very traditional Christian God.) Hence, in general, I can accept the trustworthiness of the senses which God has given to me for knowing the world. (This type of reasoning which is typically mathe-matical and a priori is sometimes called rationalism. In effect it "makes" reality conform to the rules of the mind, rather than the rules of the mind conform to reality.)

Self to God to World

Descartes has now given us the outlines of his system. We begin with the idea of the *self* (which, in essence, is a mind or a thinking thing), we proceed to the idea of God (an idea of an infinite being other than the self or the world), and eventually we come to the idea of matter of the world (which, in essence, is extension). In a very real sense, the first and central most idea in Descartes' system is the notion of God. While the idea of "Self" may be first psychologically, it is the God idea that underlines the entire enterprise. Self—to God—to the world! A roundabout way to get to the world you might remark. And indeed it is a circuitous route which Descartes has taken. But it is a path in which he has the utmost confidence. Besides God, then, two principles are going to explain everything, mind and matter. Mind is fundamentally spiritual; matter or bodies are fundamentally extension, explained by and subjected only to purely mechanical laws. Clearly, mind and matter cannot join forces completely and interpenetrate each other. They are too different from each other. One might say they are worlds apart. If it is possible that they do interact, how would they do so? How can they do so? Descartes has stepped squarely into the quagmire of the body/soul problem. He has broken Humpty Dumpty and is unable to put him back together again. What is man, when both body and mind (soul) each appear to be its own substance? Remember that for Descartes, fundamentally man is mind, a soul to which a body is attached. Subsequently, philosophers were to describe Descartes' man as a "ghost in a machine."

For Descartes, then, man fundamentally is a mind, a soul to which a body is attached. Because of this view, Descartes has been accused of making man much akin to an angel—some have said, a fallen angel. In a way Descartes, instead of advancing us in philosophy, has gone back to a Platonic view of man with all its attendant problems.

Descartes tries to finesse his way around this issue by claiming that body and soul are united and that the point of contact is in the pineal gland located somewhere in the brain. It is no answer and Descartes knows it and other philosophers knew it, too. That is why none who follow Descartes held his exact position here.

Death, Influence and New Problems

Descartes' views were well received in many quarters. Eventually he even was asked by Queen Christina of Sweden to assist her in the study of philosophy. Descartes, the bachelor, obliged in 1649, but it proved too much of a change from his early army days. The good Queen had Descartes up regularly at 5 o'clock in the morning to discuss philosophy with her. This very unphilosophical habit of rising early, together with the cold weather of Sweden, led to Descartes' demise. He died shortly thereafter in 1650.

As indicated, then, Descartes started a new movement in philosophy, for which reason he is called the father of modern philosophy. That movement is called *rationalism*. Of course, we should not hold him responsible for all of his philosophical illegitmate children!

Philosophy now began to proceed with a study of mind, before a study of matter was made. Yet Descartes could verify the external world of matter only through his having demonstrated the existence of an undeceiving God.

It should be clear what would happen if one accepted Descartes' principles, but invalidated his proof for God. If God is Descartes' bridge to the real world, He is also Descartes' Achilles' heel. Not to be able to prove that existence of God is not to have access to the real material world. This easily leads to *solipsism*, the position that all I can know is my own consciousness.

One might start with the self, but one could never get beyond the self, either. This was the path taken by some subsequent philosophers. They were logically forced to deny the material world or else make it a product of mind. They were idealist and *rationalist*.

Others preferred to accept the principles of matter as explaining everything, instead of mind. They in turn were forced to deny mind or to make it a function of matter. In general, this was the view of *empiricism*. Either way, Descartes' dualism of matter and mind set the theme and problems for thinkers in the centuries to follow.

RENÉ DESCARTES

Review Questions

1. Descartes wanted philosophy to imitate what discipline? (One in which he was famous.)
2. Was Descartes basically a rationalist or empiricist? Give the grounds for your choice.
3. Does the technique of "methodic doubt" indicate Descartes was a sceptic? Why or why not?
4. Is human error basically the fault of intellect or will for Descartes?
5. How does my doubt of my existence demonstrate that I exist?
6. Does Descartes hold that all knowledge is from the senses or that man has some innate ideas?
7. Restate the gist of Descartes' "ontological argument."
8. Descartes talks of the self, external world and God. Which of these comes first, second and third in what he knows for certain?
9. Why cannot there be a perfect or substantial unity between mind and matter as principles which make up man?
10. Why is Descartes termed the "father of modern philosophy?"

Special Thought Question

Is it possible (and if so, how) that matter and mind can influence each other if both are so different from each other? If they are subject to the same laws, can they be different? If they are not different, is mind fundamentally matter, or is matter fundamentally spiritual (mind)?

BIBLIOGRAPHY

Primary Source: The Meditations and Selection from the Principles. Tr. by John Veitch (LaSalle: Open Court Publishing Co., 1950). (The Meditations carry out Descartes' Method and the Principles summarizes these.)

Secondary Source: Descartes. S. V. Keeling, 2nd Edition (London: Oxford University Press, 1968). (A classic study of the time, influence and philosophy of Descartes.)

7
DAVID HUME (1711-1776)

"Generally speaking, the errors in religion are dangerous; those in philosophy only ridiculous." Treatise on Human Nature

Scepticism Revisited

Rationalism and Empiricism

If rationalists put their trust in reason and felt that truth was easy to come by, the empiricists put theirs in sense and hoped at best only for probability. Rationalists tended to be optimists, e.g., Leibniz' "best possible world." Such a world was quickly dismissed by Voltaire on the occasion of the great Lisbon earthquake which killed thousands of people.

Empiricists regarded themselves as the only true realists. Typical among these was the political philosopher, Thomas Hobbes. In his *Leviathan*, he argued that in the state of nature, presocietal man lived in a "nasty and brutish" world. Man was a *homo homini lupos*, a wolf seeking to devour every other. The only way to keep men from killing each other was to have all surrender their power to one ruler whose power then would be absolute. Such a one would keep the peace. Thus it came about that society was formed.

Empiricists were content to settle for experience and to live within it. Rationalists felt that by sheer *tour de force* of mind, they somehow could transcend experience. If Descartes was the prince of the rationalists, David Hume standing on the shoulders of Hobbes, could be awarded that title for the empiricists.

Some Writings and Reputation

David Hume was born in Edinburgh, Scotland, in 1711. Reared in a strict Calvinistic tradition, he attended the University of Edinburgh and studied a variety of subjects. Despite his interest in law, history and economics,

Hume always found himself getting back to questions concerning religion and philosophical problems. As a matter of fact, one of the last of his writings was his *Two Essays on Suicide and Immortality*. Some of his other writings were various essays on *Morals* and one on the *Natural History of Religion*.

Now as we know, the eighteenth century was the heyday of the great successes of Sir Isaac Newton. David Hume thought that he would try to apply the methods of experimental philosophy, i.e. Newtonian science, to moral subjects. But his outspokenness and frank expressions proved to be rather shocking to his contemporaries, especially when applied to the area of morals and ethics. He held that the basis of morality and religion was natural and rooted in man rather than in the supernatural. (This is simply one more indication of the humanism of the Enlightenment period.) Although some viewed Hume's ideas as almost refreshing in an age of lettered hypocrisy, his reputation as "horrid atheist" and sceptic was enough to prevent the staid University of Edinburgh from giving him a Professorship.

The charge that he was a sceptic probably stemmed from the book which he wrote in France. It was called *A Treatise on Human Nature*. Human nature, thought Hume, was the most basic study, yet it was often the most neglected. Apparently, it was to *stay* neglected for some time, because as Hume described it, the book fell "stillborn from the press." In this work as well as in subsequent revisions, Hume attempted to discover if we can know anything for certain. He wanted to determine the limitations of our knowledge.

Some Tough Questions

Hume had been unhappy with the claims of the rationalists who like spiders spun many theories out of their own innards, theories which Hume felt could never be validated in the real order. Increasingly, Hume began to follow the footsteps of those who saw that man's knowledge is severely restricted.

Philosophers from Plato to Descartes had claimed to know the essences of things, their substantial natures as opposed to the merely accidental and phenomenal aspects they reveal. In effect, they claimed to know what an onion *is* rather than just knowing what its characteristics are, e.g., round, whitish-yellow, hard, etc. The essence was its internal nature, something hidden beneath these qualities that only constitute its appearances. Hume felt this view unwarranted. Although he allowed for man's ability to generalize, he did not agree that we are able to abstract the essences from things. In fact, we cannot know what, if anything, i.e., the substance or essence, lies beneath these appearances present in experience. Hume seriously doubts Descartes "ghost in the machine." Man was what appeared, no more or less. Man was what could be experienced about him, nothing more. Indeed, were we to peel an onion in order to get at its innermost essence or nature, all we would find there—is more peels! In short, an onion is nothing more than its peels, and this is all we can hope to know. This says it all. Should we dare to say this was *unappealing* to the rationalists?

Personal Identity

Hume even had the courage to apply this position to knowledge about the self. We often use language which talks about the ego, self or soul as though it is something which underlies our regular activities. For example, we say, "I caught myself thinking about. . . . " Or, "I found myself dozing off. . . . " Both statements seem to suggest that there are two selves—the one that was caught and the other. But what evidence is there, other than the pitfalls of language, to support the position that there is *any* self at all. No self? Now that is a radical position. One can discern immediately what an unsettling effect Hume had on his contemporaries. Undaunted, Hume continues. Perhaps we are nothing more than the thought we think—a bundle of images or thoughts and feelings only. Does language mislead us to think something is there that isn't there? Even a cursory glance shows that language often seems to imply something that isn't. For example, in the sentence, "It has been a long time since I saw you," does the "It" stand for anything? Or does it simply repeat the same reality as "long time?" Let's try to make this clearer through use of another example.

Perhaps the "self" is like the word, "universe." The universe is simply a noun conveniently used to indicate the totality of things in existence. If things completely ceased to be, the universe would cease to be, for *the universe is only the things it "contains."* (For this reason, there is nothing *outside* the universe, for if something exists, by definition, it must be "in" the universe, since that is the way we use the term in language.)

Still another example, since that's the way we eventually can grasp a principle. Is water *in* the river, or *is* water the river? Are water and the river two realities separate and distinct or only the same thing described by different words? Are persons *in* the army, or are persons (taken together in a certain way and under certain circumstances) the army? Again, to one who is unknowing, one would think that the morning star, the evening star and the planet Venus are three different realities. In fact they all are one and the same. Now we can ask the question again, "Are ideas in the mind or are ideas the mind itself?"

Getting back to the mind, perhaps it is a fallacy due to the misuse of language then, rather than a rationalistic insight, that makes us insist on a distinction between consciousness and the objects (ideas) it is said to contain.

After all, when I am conscious, I am always conscious of something. Consciousness never can be aware of itself apart from an object present to it. I never experience myself as self, but only as hot or cold or hungry or thirsty. There simply is no empirical evidence, says Hume, that mind is anything other than its content.

Hume feels he has cut the ground out from any argument of substances underlying the appearances and accidental qualities of things. Basically they are only what we perceive them to be. This is of especial concern to the problem of one's own personal identity. One might ask whether someone now at the age of 50 is the same person he was forty five years ago. His answer probably would be "Yes" and "No," not unusual for a philosopher, we might add. He has certainly changed in appearance, he weighs more, has lost more hair, etc. Yet he will want to maintain that essentially he still is the same human being. Hume would have no problem with this as a matter of belief, but the question is whether or not it can be speculatively verified, that is, warranted theoretically. If one has a brick outhouse on one's vacation property and if over a period of years each brick and board has been replaced by other bricks and boards, could it still be considered the same outhouse? Do we, as humans even have the same body, since with the exception of some brain cells, each cell has been replaced over a period of time? If mind is nothing more than its ideas, than can man be anything more than process, since these ideas are always changing? This reminds one of the reflection of a philosopher in ancient times. His name was Heraclitus and he is reputed to have said, "No man can step into the same stream twice." His disciple, Cratylus, as is wont with most disciples, outdid him by declaring, "No man can step into the same stream once!"

The only way I could affirm evidential basis for self identity is to have experienced this through an impression. But the "I" never experiences a pure self. As indicated earlier, it only experiences itself as hot or cold, sad or happy, etc. Reversing Berkeley's position, *"Esse est percepti"*, i.e., to be is to be perceived, Hume could claim that "To be is to perceive." To say that I am the same person I was yesterday fundamentally is an assumption. No proof can be garnered for it. The assumption rests on resemblance, and imagination, rather than experience bridges the gap between two discrete moments uniting the two as one. An example will be of help. Let us say we are watching one of the cowboy movies made by John Wayne near the end of his life. On the screen, we see him almost struggle to get up on his horse and then we see him ride off lickety-split in the distance. We identify through imagination that the person who got up on his horse and the person who is riding away are the same. Why? It is because they look the same. In fact, they are two different persons, John Wayne and his stand-in—or in the case of the horse rider, his sit-in.

On another tack we see the language difficulties we can get into regarding the problem of identity. Let us say I view a corpse and claim it is the body of my friend. Can it be such? Can there even be a dead man here? If there is a man, i.e., an organism, by definition, he is not dead. The decomposing corpse is not a dead man. Can we even say it was his body, since it no longer is organic. With such subtlety and twists, we can understand how modern language philosophers have tried to *exhume* Hume, looking to him for support for their positions.

Theory of Knowledge

Having raised such philosophically embarrassing questions, Hume now tries to ascertain how, if at all, an acceptable method might be employed to cope with them. Perhaps such problems are even best not solved, but dissolved, through a better and more proper use of language. Even the twentieth century philosopher, Ludwig Wittgenstein, once declared, "Language is like clothes; it both can reveal and conceal!"

Hume starts his quest for such clarification by noting that our knowledge deals with two types of *perception*. These differ more in degree than in kind. The first may be termed *impressions* and their source is sensation or reflection. The experiences of colors, temperatures and desires would be appropriate examples. The second kind of perceptions we enjoy may be termed *ideas* and basically these are secondhand copies of the former, stemming from memory or imagination. Examples might be substance or the concept of cause. Obviously, both types of perception may be simple or a combination of many perceptions rolled into one. Heat is a simple impression whereas *Medusa* is a complex idea.

Now the ultimate test of the validity of perception is whether or not we can trace it back to an impression derived from sensory experience. That is, unless we can trace the idea or image back to an initial sensory experience, that idea or image has no claim to truth. Experience, then, as given to the senses is the final arbiter of truth. What cannot be experienced cannot be claimed and verified as true. It is important to realize that we know only the experience. What the nature of the reality that is the source of that experience remains forever beyond our ken.

Since our ideas are copies, they are immediately suspect, although some, especially those simples ones from memory, may stand the test of traceability to experience and therefore truth. Impressions, being closer to raw experience, are more trustworthy, although the complex ones must be investigated.

Hume's response to the rationalist then, is that although we may claim to have ideas such as God, soul, self, immortality, etc., the fact that these are not traceable to experience (as well as their very lack of vividness, which normally marks all impressions) shows that they are not valid.

We should note well Hume's substitution of "vividness" for Descartes "clear and distinct." Descartes' criteria are fundamentally intellectual; Hume's are sensual.

This examination of our sensory knowledge, then, demonstrates that all we really can know are phenomena or appearances. There being no sense image of an essence, I have no grounds to assert that there are such realities as essences and natures. For this reason, Hume is regarded as a nominalist, one for whom the word "essence" is just that—a name, a word, nothing more.

Analytic vs. Synthetic Propositions

But there is still one fundamental point of rationalism which Hume must attack to make his case convincing. That is the problem of causality. When someone claims that his knowledge goes beyond (transcends) his sensory experience (which Hume of course denies is possible) the claim is based on the assertion that an effect demands a cause and so one can reason from a seen effect to an unseen cause, as for example, the argument for God from order in the world. We do not see Him, only His effects. These, however, through the chain of causality, allow us to infer or deduce His experience.

The entire point though is whether through thought alone, one somehow can deduce existence. Descartes claimed this, but the key points of rationalism are pretty well rebutted by the hard Scottish philosopher. Propositions are of two types says Hume. These are *analytic* and *synthetic*. An example of an analytic proposition is "My brother is a member of my family." This can be seen to be true merely by analyzing the meaning of the terms. They reveal that the predicate term "member of family" is already implicit in the subject term, "My brother." This is why we smile at the contradictory remark, "My brother is an only child!" In effect, the former is a tautology and says simply that "A is A." (The latter says "A is non-A.") Geometry contains analytic propositions such as "A triangle contains 180 degrees." "Circles are round."

On the other hand, a synthetic proposition is, "Some houses have smoke detectors." No analysis of the subject term "some houses" reveals "the predicate term "smoke detectors." The only way I can know that some houses have smoke detectors is to go to "some houses" and find out if this is true. I determine the truth of this statement, that is, the connection between subject and predicate, by checking it out with reality.

Another example of a synthetic proposition is, "The coffee pot is hot." I cannot deduce that it is so by thinking about the meaning of the terms (analytic); I must actually sense the fact. The proposition about a triangle having 180 degrees contains a necessity—a logical necessity put there by definition and the meaning of terms. But though it has necessity (put into it, so to speak), it does not add to my storehouse of information about the real world. It gives me no newness. The proposition that the coffee pot is hot does give me information and newness about the world. After all, before I touched it, I didn't know its heat as an existential fact. But the coffee pot didn't have to be hot; it could have been cold. Hence, while I gain knowledge, I lose necessity, for such synthetic propositions are always contingent, according to Hume. In short, we can't have newness and necessity. We can't have a proposition both analytic and synthetic. (Kant will have something to say about this later, but that's where it stands for now.)

When all is said and done, according to Hume the only way I could have of knowing (vs. believing) that God exists, is if I can sense this in my experience. Although many such claims constantly are made, when the chips are down, there is no public evidence that anyone has had a direct and immediate experience of God. Such claims are unverified and for Hume, unverifiable in principle. Thus, to say, "God spoke to me in a dream," and to say that "I dreamt God spoke to me," amount to one and the same statement as far as public evidence is concerned.

Other aspects of language also need clarification. To tell a child that "If you don't go to sleep, the Boogie Man will get you," conveys no information whatsoever. It is not a statement which conveys information, so much as it is one that tries to promote a response, i.e., to have the child go to sleep. In short, it is an *emotive* and not a *cognitive* statement. A statement no different from this is, "If you don't obey me, God will punish you." It reveals no information that there is a God; it only wants the child to obey.

The Problem of Causality

Bearing these distinctions in mind, let us pick up again on how they relate to the problem of causality. Hume's answer here is historic and consequential. Philosophers long have maintained that "Whatever comes to be demands a cause." Is this an analytic or synthetic proposition? That is the question and on it rides the possibility for scientific truth. It is not analytic, says Hume, for in no way can I squeeze out the concept of "cause" from the notion of "what comes to be." (I may associate the two, but we'll examine that later; it is of no import for this issue.) The proposition, if not analytic, then must be synthetic. Accordingly, it must give newness, add something to the subject term and be able to have its claim checked out in experience. Hume now takes a close look at whether it is experientially verifiable, by proceeding to make a close inspection of the nature of causality and its claims.

Causality is a complex idea (vs. a simple one) and therefore contains several elements which must be separated and tested for traceability to experience, if it is to be understood as true. According to Hume, cause contains the implication that *it is prior to the effect* (as it would have to be, in order to bring something into existence). It must be *contiguous* with the effect, that is, in direct or indirect contact with the effect. The cause and effect sequence is invariable and the connection a necessary one. Given these conditions, let's test the validity of the concept of causality according to Hume's methodology.

Take the instance of fire and getting heated or burned by it. Every time I approach fire, I experience heat or warmth. In stepping back, I no longer experience this heat. No matter how many times I do this, the results are the same. Thus, much of what the principle of causality implies, namely, priority, contiguity and invariable sequence, is validated in the sensory experience. For a moment, it looks like we are home free, for three fourths of the requirements already are met.

But, asks Hume, do I discover in the sensory experience the *necessary connection* between cause and effect which is so essential to causality? Here Hume searches for an affirmative answer but can find none. Each sensory experience is only that of an unnecessary or contingent singular. What is it that justifies one in thinking as do we all, that the next time I approach the fire, I will become heated again? This seems to be a necessary way of thinking, yet I cannot ground such necessity in the sense experience which grasps only the contingent each time. The resolution Hume gives to this problem is one for which he is famous. Academically it is shocking and scandalous, for he denies us the only way we have to escape the confines of experience to get to the metaphysical "beyond" of the rationalists.

According to Hume, the reason I get the idea of necessary condition (one that is absolutely vital to the concept causality) is due to custom or habit and nothing else. The only reason I begin to assert that this is the cause of that, is due to my experience of *repeated* acts, of one following upon the other, the first being called "cause" and the second, "effect." Repetition, then, not some kind of experiential insight into necessity is responsible for my thinking "necessity" and attributing it to the sequence I have witnessed. The grounds for the necessity must lie *not in the single object or instance of supposed causality*, but in the repetition itself, this engenders a psychological association, such that when I experience C (cause) I will experience E (effect). (As an aside, we recall how Pavlov's dog responded to the clang of the bell by salivating, expecting that food would accompany its ringing, as it did on previous occasions. He now salivated without the food, simply upon hearing the bell. Similarly, as one philosopher explained, a peasant may have thought that the rooster was the cause of the dawn since every time it crowed, the sun started coming up!)

To sum up, the causal inference depends upon the association of ideas, instead of the reverse as had been the previous and mistaken notion. Partly, this is why modern day advertising is based almost exclusively on repetition and association, rather than on causality. In advertising, it is a truism that pretty girls sell cars, yet there is no causal connection between the pretty girl and the car. Of course we may dream up some such connections, but these are in the mind, not in reality.

An example will clarify this. In the movies we see a big fight scene. We cringe as our favorite actor gets struck by the bad guy's fist and goes reeling. Then the sequence is reversed and our hero floors his opponent with a mighty blow to the chin. Imaginatively, we are willing to accept the association of sequences as examples of causality, BUT IN FACT we know that there was only sequence and no causality. Our actors did not reel *from* the blows. By prearrangement, when the one threw a "punch," the other fell back, neither even touching the other, or if doing so, only lightly.

Perhaps a better example is that of a pedestrian waiting at a traffic light. He sees a button telling him to push it to change the light in his favor that he might cross. He presses the button, the light changes and he assumes that it changed *because* he pressed the button. The assumption is not validated, however, for there was no experience of a necessary connection between his action and what happened. Only sequence was experienced. One can even imagine a repair man coming along saying that the button hasn't worked for months and he was there now to fix it. Would the pedestrian still claim that the button "worked?"

It is noteworthy that Hume often has been misunderstood on this issue. He was not denying the concept of causality as useful and having practical benefits; he simply held that the concept is not speculatively verifiable, this to the consternation of many! This implies then that in our quest for knowledge, we can never get beyond the realm of probability. We cannot attain certitude as preached by legions of philosophers before now. The truth is—truth is not attainable, in any strict sense of the term.

Instinct and Belief

For Hume, it would be much better for man to place his trust in instinct and belief rather than in speculative thought which is forever unverifiable. Reason must take a back seat to the two. This especially is the case in practical matters where our passions do and should dominate our life, rather than reason. To prove his point he gives the example of a man who has welded an iron cage and hangs it over a cliff. He knows that there is no danger of it falling and dashing on the ground, for he has triple checked his workmanship. Nonetheless, if he gets inside the suspended cage, his rational convictions will be cast aside and he will fear for his life.

Philosophy and religion now take a new turn. Since one can't deduce matters of fact, that is, reach the existential order through anything but sensation, attention began to focus on the nature of belief. This was a "gut" feeling that something was true.

Belief, says Hume, "raises" the level of an idea to that of an impression. This enables us to feel that some things are true even though we *cannot know* that to be the case. To exemplify, I cannot know my friend is the same person (has the same identity) as he was the last time we met. But my strong belief is that such is the case. I cannot shake that belief, even though I know it cannot be verified in any technical sense.

These views of Hume provided the basis of the nature of religion for the great Protestant culture philosopher, Schliermacher. Religion amounted to a feeling of absolute dependence. John Wesley, founder of Methodism, also referred to "the heart strangely warmed."

Not only in religion, but in morality itself, feeling became the criterion by which an act was judged moral or immoral. When we witness certain acts with which we have an affinity or instinctive sympathy, we call them "good acts." When we witness other acts and they evoke in us an antipathy, we call them "bad acts." There formed around this position an entire school of philosophers called the Scottish Common Sense School. Moral sentiment was its *leit motiv.* To sum up, there is no speculative verification of the "ought" of morality. Philosophically all I know is the "is" of actions. Speculatively, all actions appear as value-free to knowledge. One can never derive the "ought" from the "is," hence morality needs a new foundation, that of "feeling."

An Appraisal

In all fairness to Hume, it can be said that he himself saw that his position came to a dead-end, for scepticism is a kind of intellectual suicide. However, he openly confesses that he can't see how he can extricate himself from it, desirable as that might be.

Despite his philosophical views—or perhaps because of them—David Hume had enjoyed a certain popularity with the high society of the times. He befriended Rousseau in France and later entertained Rousseau for some time at his home in London. However it did not prove to be a lasting friendship. Hume was also in contact with the other intellectuals of the time, among them, Diderot, Helvetius, and especially Adam Smith of Edinburgh, who wrote the famous book, *The Wealth of Nations*.

All his life, Hume was a man of controversy. Even on his deathbed, when Johnson's biographer, Boswell, questioned Hume about immortality, Hume replied that it was pure nonsense.

Oddly enough, although Hume is known and studied primarily by philosophers today, his claim to fame in his own times was more due to works that he had written on economics and especially history, the latter causing a political furor. Today, the school of linguistic analysis has rediscovered Hume and his thoughts once again prove perennially provocative.

If the importance of a man's ideas is proportionate to the influence he had on others, Hume was and remains a towering figure.

DAVID HUME

Review Questions

1. Name one book of Hume's and the century in which he lived.
2. Hume belonged to the empiricist camp in philosophy. Basically what is empiricism?
3. Why or why not would Hume agree with Descartes' notion of self as "thinking substance?"
4. Which is more true and basic—intellectual or sensory knowledge?
5. What is the test by which I can determine if an idea is true?
6. Hume is a nominalist regarding natures or essences of things. Explain.
7. In causality, the so-called necessary connection is grounded not on insight but on repetition (custom or habit) and association, according to Hume. Explain what this means.
8. What are the implications for science, given the above (Question 7) as true?
9. Which is the more important for Hume, instinct or reason? Why?
10. In what way was Hume a representative of the Enlightenment Period?

Special Thought Question

How must I define experience to hold on the one hand, that I cannot get beyond experience, and on the other, to claim that I am able to transcend experience?

BIBLIOGRAPHY

Primary Source: *A Treatise on Human Nature.* Ed. by L. A. Selley-Bigge (London: Oxford University Press, 1951). (The most basic of Hume's many works.)

Secondary Source: *The Philosophy of David Hume.* Normon Smith Kemp (London: MacMillan, 1960). (A well known survey of Hume's ideas.)

8
IMMANUEL KANT (1720–1804)

"There is nothing that can without restriction be considered good, except only a good will." Foundations of the Metaphysics of Morals

The Philosophical Revolution

Often, those who influence thought and cultures, like ocean undertows, remain hidden from open view. Yet their effect is unmistakably felt by all who venture into the depths. There are names in history known to all—Plato, Columbus, Napoleon, but there are also names of historical significance known to but few—Hippocrates, Charles Martel, Enrico Fermi. Immanuel Kant may be numbered among the latter. His ideas have had profound influence on the Western world in philosophy, science and religion. Here in America, they provided a framework for the Protestant frontier West. Until missionaries and churches came along, Kant's morality dominated the Western pioneers.

Like Copernicus, he sought to effect a reversal of the established order in the three disciplines mentioned. He used philosophy in an attempt to demonstrate that its inner core of metaphysics was never and could never be legitimized. He told science that nature and its laws were not revealed so much *to* man, but prescribed, dictated and superimposed on nature *by* man. He replaced religion out of which an ethic arose, with an ethic out of which religion arose. He was a mathematician, scientist and a philosopher. He was also a humanist. He was, in the words of Moses Mendelsshohn, "the great system crusher and destroyer."

Life and Times

Immanuel Kant was born in Koenigsberg in East Prussia in 1724. He lived his entire life in that university town and died there in 1804. The eighty years which spanned his life were a momentous period in the history of the West, for Kant was a product of the eighteenth century, the Age of Enlightenment.

This was the time of increased belief in the dignity of man and his right to determine his own patterns of destiny. It was the age of self-reliance and the era of Rousseau's "noble savage" and the French Revolution, of Ben Franklin and the American Declaration of Independence. It was an epoch ushered in by John Locke's *Reasonableness of Christianity* and marked by the wit and satire of a Voltaire. The rationalism of Leibniz and Wolff held sway, as did the "Invisible Hand" of the economics of Adam Smith. The exuberance of the times were tempered only by the scepticism of David Hume.

In part, Kant reflected all of these diversities of the age. His own background of Protestant Pietism (an anticlerical movement among the German Lutherans) certainly exercised a good measure of influence on his development in later life. The son of a saddlemaker, Kant attended the University of Koenigsberg and studied philosophy and mathematics. However, his interest in physics, which thanks to Newton had now come of age, and theology were widespread as well.

Kant's life was as typically methodical as his writings. His afternoon walks were nearly always taken at the same time. As some remarked, one could set one's watch by Kant's habits. The only time the routine was broken was when Rousseau's *Emile*, which Kant had been anxiously awaiting, arrived by the mails.

Up to about 1770, Kant lived the life of a private tutor and low ranking instructor at Koenigsberg. His quick wit made him a favorable companion and up to now, he could be regarded as quite the "gay blade." In 1770 he received a Professorship to the Chair of Logic and Mathematics. It is almost with this appointment that Kant's life goes into its long second phase.

Prior to this date, Kant (in philosophy) had been subjected almost exclusively to the strong influence of the rationalists. This tradition had as its chief representatives, Leibniz, Wolff and a man who taught Kant at Koenigsberg, Schultz. Kant's own works up to this time were few in number. Most were concerned with science. This period in Kant's life has been known as his pre-critical period, for as he himself tells us, he accepted rationalistic philosophy on a rather dogmatic and unquestioning basis.

It is at this juncture in Kant's career that he became more and more concerned with the empiricism and scepticism of David Hume, even though he had been aware of these earlier. To say that Hume's ideas came as a shock to Kant is a gross understatement. Hume's ideas pricked the bubble of Kant's dream world. As Kant himself was to declare, Hume "awakened me from my dogmatic slumber." At the time, Kant felt himself caught in a crossfire. His own sympathies lay with accepting the validity and objectivity of Newtonian physics and science and he was naturally disposed to accept the systematic rationalistic philosophy of the day. Yet Hume's criticism of science and rationalism was so great that Kant could not ignore it. Indeed, a thoroughgoing investigation of the problems which Hume posed was going to be a major part of Kant's life work. Kant, of course, did not realize this at the time, for he tells us that as early as 1772, he hoped to complete his book entitled *The Critique of Pure Reason* in three months. In fact, however, it took him nine more years.

A Change of Perspective

Let's see if we can pose the problems which Kant saw facing him. Prior to Hume's influence on Kant, Kant accepted without question the validity, the universality, and the necessity of Newtonian science. He accepted, too, the method of philosophizing which has been handed down by the rationalistic tradition. In the main, this was a method which all but ignored the sensory order of things. For the most part, rationalism was content to deduce from the mind the basic structure of reality.

Now it was Hume's contention that scientific knowledge, as previously described, was impossible. For Hume, no judgments have necessity and universality. Causality is nothing else than an association of ideas arising largely from custom of habit.

Kant was quick to see that if Hume were correct, there could be no science in the strict sense of the term, for certitude would be reduced to a kind of probability at best. Thus Kant's *Critique of Pure Reason* is a rebuttal and an effort to justify the basis of Newtonian science, thereby showing it to be valid. This Kant felt he was able to do by indicating that science legitimately uses universal and necessary propositions, but only in the phenomenal realm, the order of appearance, the only order accessible to science anyways.

In short, Newtonian science *could* attain its object, i.e., the world of phenomena, and thus have a sensory and empirical basis. In addition, the mind would supply certain categories of universality and necessity to give such knowledge its scientific flavor. Thus Kant synthesized the Newtonian requirements of incorporating the empirical and mental sides of experience. Yet this was accomplished at a considerable cost. For Kant had to claim that laws, causality, universality and similar categories are not discovered in reality, rather these are imposed upon it, thereby helping to organize it and to make it scientific. In short, the laws of science are not *discovered* in the real order but are *imposed* upon the real order, through the structuring activities of mind. Laws, then, are *prescribed* by mind. This was Kant's own *Copernican* Revolution. The knower did not revolve around things any longer, rather, things revolved around the knower.

To put it differently, things do not exist in *space* or in *time* for Kant. Rather, the reason we must always interpret reality as through space-time categories, is because they are part of our make-up. Thus, space and time are always (universality) the windows of the senses through which all information must (necessity) pass for it to be known. Space and time do not belong to things—they belong only to the knower. Accordingly, universality and necessity belong only to the knower as well.

Science as Valid, Metaphysics as Invalid

Having solved the problem which Hume posed with respect to science, Kant now tackled the difficulty of philosophical knowledge, especially that of the possibility of metaphysics (the very heart and soul of philosophy). Could metaphysics stand the test of science? To claim it was scientific, it had to submit itself to this examination. Now we recall that for Kant, two requirements are necessary for science: (1) science must be able to attain its object or that which it deals with, and (2) the mind must have certain categories or ideas which will unify and systematize the material, giving it a scientific status. Mathematics and the physical sciences were able to meet these requirements, but what of metaphysics?

True, we have categories or ideas (ideals) of God, the Soul, Freedom, the World and so on. Hence, the latter half of the requirement for science can be met. But now comes the crucial point. Metaphysics and philosophy claim to go beyond (transcend) ordinary science in that they purport to deal not with appearances or *phenomena*, but with the very heart of reality, with the *noumenal* order of the thing in itself! This, Kant claims, is impossible. For to know a thing, we must change it, that is, filter it through our categories or ways of knowing. Hence *we can never know that thing as it is in itself*, but only as it has been refined by us in the knowing or transmuting process. It's like asking, "How do you know your refrigerator light is off?" Well, the reply might be, "I'll open the door to find out!" Ah! But in so doing you are changing the conditions and sure enough, when you open the door, you'll see the light is not off but ON!

Let's make this point as clear as possible, for it is crucial to an understanding of Kant's insights. There is on the market a toothpaste which when it is squeezed from the tube onto the toothbrush is striped. Most persons think nothing of this, brush their teeth and are through with the ritual. However, a philosophically minded person will be curious and wonder if the toothpaste is striped *in the tube* or only when it *flows out of the tube*. Now let us presuppose for sake of argument, that there were no way to cut or break into the tube, to see how the toothpaste was arranged there. Would one ever know for sure if the way the paste came out of the tube, i.e., striped, was the same way it was in the tube? Since we could see the paste only *after* we squeezed it out of the tube most likely we would think that it must be the same way in the tube, i.e., striped. But may we make such an assumption? On the other hand, may we make the assumption that it isn't in the tube the same way as it comes out of the tube? The Kantian answer to both questions is that neither assumption is permitted! We will always be tempted to make assumptions but that's all they will ever be, unverified assumptions.

As an upshot to all of this, it becomes clear that we can only know what appears (phenomena) and not what, if anything, is behind the appearance in the realm of the thing in itself (noumenon). Now the above is an analogy only and like most analogies, it limps a bit, but it does make its point.

Because metaphysics could never attain its object in reality, that is, God, World, Soul, it can never lay claim to the character of science as certain knowledge. Kant felt that we must always be on our guard against this seductive tendency of our mind to commit this error of giving metaphysics scientific status. He even suggests that this tendency may have been put in us to humble us. The best we are able to do in philosophy is to discover the limits of our mind and this Kant feels he has done. It remains for others to explore and map out the interior.

Religion and Morality

There was yet another problem which needed explanation and that was the problem of faith and reason. Here Kant's attitude was evident when he wrote in the preface to his *Critique of Pure Reason* that his aim was "to deny knowledge to make room for faith."

In some respects, this perhaps is what Kant may well have considered as his greatest contribution, although not all have agreed with him on this matter. Kant felt that the world of science was a world of necessity, a world of determined and mechanical causes which brook no exception. Such a world permitted no freedom. Hence Kant sought to carve out a second world which would be more favorable to the climate of faith, morality and religion. Without freedom such a world could not exist. This new world, so to speak, he places in the area and concern of the will, or, as he terms it, in the order of practical reason, instead of theoretical reason which governs the Newtonian world of science. Since the two worlds have been separated in this fashion, each like a boxer standing in his own corner and never venturing out into the ring, they cannot attack each other. An assault on faith by science will be fruitless and vice versa, for they have nothing to say to each other and nothing to do with each other. They are simply two ships passing in the dark night.

Kant's philosophy thus culminates in a modified dualism, keeping two orders apart from each other, one to deal with science and knowledge, the other with faith and action. Yet Kant came dangerously close to creating a morality bereft of content and of fashioning a religion on a wholly natural basis. His views of these matters came under sharp attack in Prussia and he was forbidden to publish them.

Briefly, these views might be summarized as follows. Traditionally, the morality of an action was regarded as determined by three factors: (1) the act itself, e.g., murder as intrinsically wrong, almsgiving as intrinsically good; (2) the circumstances which surround it, e.g., infanticide, homocide, patricide, assassination and (3) the intention of the agent performing the act, e.g., do I give alms for the help of others or because I expect them to vote for me in an election. In order for an action to be morally good, all three requirements must be met. To be bad, only one requirement could be absent. In short, morality and religion (the two are identical for Kant) seemed to be based on external laws and criteria.

Given man's dignity, however, suggests Kant, which is more meaningful—a law imposed from above or one steming from my inner self? Can I claim that my action is moral if it is done for the sake of something external such as a reward? Can I call my action virtuous if I refrain from extra-marital sex because I am afraid of catching venereal disease? Is true religion one of currying favor and grovelling before the Almighty, or one of the ethical life?

Kant's answer is clear. Just as knowledge revolves around the knower, so morality must revolve around the dignity of the human person. That dignity demands that moral law must not be from above or outside but generated from within myself. Accordingly, in generating the law myself, I preserve my autonomy as a human person. Thus I am not only a subject of the law, but its very legislator as well. Additionally, I freely bind myself to that law and so emulate the ideal of self-government. It was made to order for a democratic New World.

In short, the goodness or morality of an act will now no longer be from without but solely from within. That goodness will be determined by one thing and one thing only, the intention of the agent. What must that intention be? It may not be relative and subjective, for this is the destruction of all morality. No, it must be universal and objective, the same for all mankind. Yet the intention still must be generated internally; it still must come from the agent. That intention is to act for the sake of *duty!* I act morally only when I act out of duty. This is the famed categorical imperative of Kant. Hence, a will in conformity with duty will be a good will; being a good will, accordingly marks the act proceeding from it as good. This position is sometimes called ethical formalism or de-ontological ethics. I do not act for the sake of happiness, although happiness may accompany the action. Yet I must be careful that my concern for happiness does not get in the way of my sense of duty. Duty, then, sought for its own sake can be applied universally to all moral actions of all humans. To the extent that each does his duty, immorality will disappear.

But how does one judge what is one's duty? The answer is that one must ask if one's obligation would be incumbent upon all others in like circumstances. In short, what I require myself to do in duty, I should be able to ask of others as well.

Put more in Kant's own words, we can formulate several ways of saying the same thing. (1) "Act in such a way that your action could serve as universal law." (2) "Act always so that you treat humanity, whether in your own person or in that of another, always as an end and never as a simple means." (3) "Act in such a way that your will could consider itself as making universal laws by its maxims."

The sense of duty almost appears somewhat Prussian in character, but Kant makes a strong case for it. It is a "pure" morality. Highly idealistic, one might question to what extent man can use it for a guideline. It becomes more reasonable if we compare it to the mathematical notion of "pi" (3.14, etc.). It can never be reached but we can always get closer to the ideal. With duty, we rely wholly upon ourselves. With duty, we respect our nature as humans. For example, a man goes into a washroom after hours, "dying" for a cigarette. He sees the sign "No Smoking." No one is around, no one will see him and he is responsible enough not to start a fire. May he "light up?" Duty would require he not do so, for the law, which he, in the person of other men, has generated, would be flouted. The principle that he may not flout the law as such, is a principle he expects others to obey as well as himself. Without it, chaos would result. Another example is the following: It is late at night and you are driving down a country road coming to a four-way Stop intersection. You have a good field of vision, you see with certainty no cars are coming and wonder whether you should continue without stopping. Duty commands you to stop for the same reason cited in the previous example. For practical purposes, this human autonomy in morality, cuts down the need for religion.

Kant's position for which he was criticized by the government is that he has paved the way for religious ethics being replaced with ethical religion. Religion henceforth will come out of ethics, not the reverse. Religion is now encouraged to follow reason rather than reason follow religion. Anything religion requires beyond good conduct, i.e., morality, is only magic and demeaning to man and God.

Freedom, Immortality and God

Completing his thought, Kant now puts back into the philosophical picture (as postulates) three ideas which he ruled out of court regarding our metaphysical ability to know. They are the ideas of freedom, immortality and God. For example, every human experiences obligation at one time or another. This sense of the "ought" is as universal as mankind itself, although we can find considerable disagreement with respect to what it is we "ought" to do. At any rate the "ought" is a given, a datum of universal experience. This would not make sense unless I postulate that I am *free*. (Note the argument goes rather backward and therefore is a *transcendental argument* in rather convoluted terminology.)

Next, I feel that I am obliged to seek continual perfection. This seems true for basically each of us wants to be a better person and we live our lives in this expectation, always working toward it in one way or another. It is equally clear that such an urge cannot be fulfilled in this life. It is too short and death is always waiting in the wings. But such perfection would be frustrated and not possible unless I continue to exist forever, thereby arguing to *immortality*. Lastly, although it is clear that virtue implies a worthiness to be happy, it does not guarantee it. Therefore, I postulate *God* as one who will join the two for me. Thus, while I cannot *know* that I am free, that my soul is immortal, or that there is a God, I can postulate and believe in all on practical grounds, since they are beyond the ability of science to pronounce upon, or metaphysics to know.

Paradoxically, it is just as well that I cannot *know* God exists. This is a good thing, since such knowledge would probably destroy all morality, the reason being that such knowledge would so overwhelm with fear of punishment or hope of reward that I could not do duty for its own sake, the only true basis for morality. It might even be said that for practical purposes, Kant's God is "freedom in the service of the ideal."

It takes but little insight to appreciate how Kant gave further impetus to his own Age of Enlightenment. That impetus was also given to the psychology of "making it on your own," especially as practiced by those who came to civilize and carve out the frontier in Western America. Those who practiced what Kant preached probably never knew his name. But we all have asked ourselves the fundamental questions Kant raised and asked of himself as a philosopher and more especially as a man. "What can I know? What must I do? What can I believe in?"

Yes, Kant is difficult to read, for he is one of the earliest to write his treatises in the German vernacular, rather than in Latin. Indeed, although Kant wrote in German, it has been said that he first has to be translated into German in order to be understood. Consequently, his style is heavy and new terms are always cropping up. Yet understanding Kant is worth all the trouble, for here was a great mind at work, whether one regards it as for well or for ill.

His most momentous contribution was to point out the structuring characteristics of mind and how we employ them in science and in everyday activity. The application of this principle of structuring is widespread, and we observe it in imposing models on reality enabling us to get a handle on it to produce human meaning. There is no Big Dipper, but through structuring individual stars, we invent a constellation whose pointer star gives us direction. There is no latitude and longitude, but by imposing such a grid, a ship can radio its position for rescue purposes.

Before man, there was only the world of nature; with man there is the structured world of culture which gives meaning to human life. It is man's domain. Both worlds are sources of inspiration. As Kant puts it, there are two things at which we can ceaselessly marvel—"the starry heavens above me and the moral law within me." Who can disagree?

IMMANUEL KANT

Review Questions

1. Kant was influenced by rationalism and empiricism. Explain in what way and by whom.
2. What is meant by the phenomenal and noumenal orders? Which only can we know?
3. The necessity and universality of scientific laws are rooted not in things, but in the categories of the human mind. Explain.
4. Why is the heart of philosophy, metaphysics, not valid according to Kant?
5. What is meant by Kant claiming that in knowledge, things revolve around the knower than the other way around?
6. How is Question 5 a "Copernican revolution" of its own?
7. Regarding morality, how does Kant effect a "second Copernican revolution?"
8. What is Kant's meaning when he says he wants to "deny knowledge to make room for faith?"
9. Does Kant have religion proceed from morality or morality from religion?
10. Why cannot happiness be the main motivation for an ethical act? What must be the *only* real motivation?

Special Thought Question

If the universe and everything in it is governed by deterministic laws, how can man be free? If man is free, are not all laws somehow upset? What do you understand by freedom?

BIBLIOGRAPHY

Primary Source: *The Philosophy of Kant.* Ed. Carl Friedrich (New York: Modern Library, 1949). (A selection of Kant's moral and political writings.)

Secondary Source: *Kant.* S. Koerner (Baltimore: Penguin Books, 1955). (Overview of Kant's three major works on Pure Reason, Practical Reason and Judgement.)

9
GEORG HEGEL (1770–1831)

"The history of the world is none other than the progress of the consciousness of freedom."
Philosophy of History

Mind Over Matter

Every philosophical period and each philosophical movement has its high point — its crest to which everything previous has led and from which everything subsequent will follow. It was so with the philosophy of Georg Hegel. His philosophy was the apex of absolute idealism. Before him was only prologue; after him, only epilogue.

Never has the world witnessed an equal in idealistic philosophy. As we know, idealistic philosophy begins with thought and explains all reality as a manifestation of thought. In some cases, it virtually deduces the way things are from the pattern which the mind conceives in itself. For example, in constructing the Table of Elements, scientists found great gaps between various elements known at the time. They were able to deduce some elements as missing and knew where these belonged later filling them in when they were discovered empirically. Another instance would be the locating of the last planet, Pluto. Astronomers did not know by seeing that such a planet existed, but deduced from mathematical considerations that such a body must be around and in a certain area. Then they trained their telescopes on the area and "discovered" the planet.

Hegel fits squarely into this place. If one could sum up Hegel's basic principle here, it is the view that whatever is real is rational (i.e., intelligible) and whatever is rational is real. Hegel saw as his life's work, the explanation (which in rationalistic philosophy is *de facto* the justification) of that principle. It was a mighty task and Hegel produced a systematic philosophy of utmost grandeur to explain it. Yet to do so, Hegel had to develop a powerful logic — an all embracing methodology. This new logic differed radically from that of Aristotle. Instead of shunning contradiction, it welcomed it, embraced it and brought it full blown into the system. It was a method which the Marxists and Communists have taken for their own, after making some revisions of it.

The doctrine of Hegel is so all encompassing and so difficult that even Hegel himself is reported to have remarked, "Of all my disciples, only one has ever understood me, and he understood me wrongly!" With this note of caution, let us take the plunge into trying to see Hegel's great ideas.

Biographical Notes

Georg Wilhelm Friedrick Hegel was born in Stuttgart, Germany, in 1770. He studied theology and philosophy at the University of Tübingen, where he exhibited a profound interest in classical philosophy. Hegel was never satisfied with seeing various parts to reality, he was rather interested in seeing a unity among the parts, a unity which would make the parts intelligible.

We can understand his wish here for one does have to see the whole picture in order to gain an appreciation of the present moment. All of us can look back on earlier times when things often happened that didn't seem to make sense at the time. Now, however, we see they were part of a pattern carrying a forward meaning. An example is an employee, who unbeknown to himself, is being groomed for a higher position. Things are connected and involve the full understanding of their relatedness to something else. A hammer for instance, cannot be understood for what it is, except in relation to a hand, an arm and the man who uses it for some specific purpose. Seen in isolation, a hammer makes no sense at all; viewed in a larger context, it becomes meaningful.

Hegel then is a global thinker who not only saw the trees, but the forest as well, the trees being the concrete and individual embodiment of the intelligible universal whole, namely the forest. Reality for him is like a jigsaw puzzle; the parts make sense, not in themselves, but only in relation to the whole.

All of us must concede how much easier it is to work such a puzzle if we first can see how it will look when completed. We do this by looking at the cover of the box which contains it. By so doing, we will know that pieces of blue cutouts should go toward the top, reflecting a sky, green pieces to the bottom showing the ground, etc.

To do philosophy then one must first envision the whole of reality and its meaning. Only then can one see relationships between what previously appeared as piecemeal. Eventually, his striving toward unity won for him the charge of developing a pantheism, the view that all is God. Among his classmates were Schelling and the poet Hölderin. Hegel was certainly influenced by them, but he was also influenced by Kant and Fichte. As a matter of fact, one scholar rightfully claims that in one of Hegel's writings, Hegel makes Christ preach the morality of Immanuel Kant.

Hegel spent the greater part of his life teaching at various institutions. He taught at Jena, about the time that Napoleon was making his conquests. He also taught at Nuremberg, Heidelberg and Berlin. He died of the cholera in 1831. Among his many writings, probably his *Science of Logic* is the most famous. Yet his *Phenomenology of the Spirit* is also well known.

The Philosophical Backdrop of Hegel's Time

We recall that Immanuel Kant, part of whose life span coincided with Hegel, attempted to unify two different movements in philosophy—two movements which had been an outcropping of Descartes. Those movements which Kant sought to put together were empiricism (the view that only sensory knowledge is valid), and rationalism (the position that the intellect can uncover within itself the structure of reality).

We can also recall that Kant fell short of unity in trying to combine these views; indeed, Kant gave rise to a dualism once more. That dualism was between sense and intellect, between appearances and things in themselves, and between faith and reason.

Hegel saw himself as the likely candidate to put Humpty Dumpty back together again and restore order and unity. It now is up to history to pass judgment on the success of his venture.

The Dialectical Method

According to Hegel, to understand all, we must understand the laws of reason, for the real is rational and the rational is real. Now the laws which govern things for Hegel are not static and inert. Rather are they dynamic, changing, evolutionary and even contradictory, perhaps. Let's take a look at mind and reality, says Hegel. Now just what is it that we see here? Well, one thing that we observe is the fact of change, which must be read as progress. Remember that historically, rationalists always have been "dreadful optimists," as the British are wont to describe them.

In analyzing this change, we see that things tend to their opposites and then they proceed to a kind of unity or synthesis. Let's make this concrete, for certainly Hegel did just that.

Don't we see, argues Hegel, that things exist in a kind of tension of

85

opposing forces? For instance, what keeps the earth in its orbit is the counteraction of two forces, centrifugal and centripetal. Or to use a more modern example, don't we find in the atom both negative and positive charges of electricity? Don't we find that the prongs of a horseshoe magnet attract other things but repel each other? Epoxy glue is another example. It consists of two parts, neither of which has sticking qualities, but which when combined produce a strong bond. If you don't mind a pun, let's take an example really *concrete*. We can take water (a *liquid*), cement (a *dust* or *powder*), and by mixing the two produce a solid (*concrete!*).

The opposition of things not only keeps reality going, but, claims Hegel, it is this very opposition and eventual interpenetration which provides for change and newness in the world. Thus for Hegel, things tend toward their opposites and then into a new unity or synthesis. The synthesis contains all the riches of the old parts, but provides something in addition as well. (In this sense, reality is like a hybrid seed continually being cross-bred for better and better results. Examples are winter wheat, seedless grapes, nectarines, etc.)

According to this view, everything is developing toward a more perfect form or expression. The world is getting better every day. But to appreciate this we need to have an overview, i.e., see the universal, and not get lost in this or that imperfect particular, i.e., the sense manifestation.

From examples like these, Hegel gradually saw his dialectical methodology develop. The opposing forces, Hegel termed "thesis" and "antithesis"; the unity of the two was called *Einheit* or "synthesis." Since everything was rational, logic could cover all, and Hegel was quick to make metaphysics reducible to a logic. But what a logic it was! It was a dynamic logic that took in everything—and even nothing! Opponents to it would not be refuted, but rather swallowed up within the system. Hence, Hegel's philosophy is often termed a pan-logism.

To take some examples of how it worked: Hegel, who had been a keen student of history, saw that the despotism of some of the Eastern nations met their opposing counterpart in the free democracy of Athenian Greece. Our own political evolution, claimed Hegel, is the synthesis of these two opposing factors and combines elements from both. That political system was close to a constitutional monarchy which embodied the elements of Christianity and which had its most perfect expression in the Germanic ideal. History, then, if viewed as a mere collection of atomic events, dates, happenings, etc., has no particular meaning. But when seen in the larger framework of the *struggle for freedom* (or putting it differently but saying the same thing, the *development of consciousness*), history now becomes intelligible. The participants in this struggle often produce results beyond their conscious intentions, guided as it were by a larger pattern. Accordingly, history is linear and progressive. (A parallel kind of thinking was evidenced in the stories of Sherlock Holmes. The great detective was not so much interested in solving only individual crimes, but always looked behind them all, for the unmistakable hand of his arch enemy, Professor Moriarity. He controlled the web of evil but never appeared overtly in it. It was he whom Holmes sought.)

To get back to our theme of dialectic, another example is taking complete freedom (as license) as the *thesis*, and opposing it to restriction as the *antithesis*. Mature freedom under the law is the *synthesis*. We must remember that freedom for Hegel is not capriciousness, but rather that which is always in full accord with reason. Indeed it seems to be reason itself, almost in the manner that for Socrates virtue was knowledge. Hegel did not hesitate to apply this method, called the Hegelian dialectic, to religion. Christianity, then, would be the by-product of opposing historical forces. Here, the *thesis* would be God, the *antithesis*, the world, and the *synthesis*, the Incarnation (that is, God-become-man). Many accepted this presentation of Christianity as a kind of *natural* history, but there would be those to oppose it later, especially a Danish thinker, Soren Kierkegaard.

Reality then, *becomes*, an *idea*, a merger of *thought* and the world. We observe raw *facts*, give them *relations* through thought and produce the unity of Idea or Spirit or *Geist*. Religion and Art, for example, are two opposing but contributing forces which develop philosophy. The great American philosopher-psychologist, William James, summed up Hegel's position here by pointing out that we secure peace by war, liberty by laws, command over nature by obedience to nature.

Emergence of Spirit

In the last analysis, it appears that all history is in the process of development. This development witnesses an unfolding of Absolute Spirit or Mind. Put more simply, we find that the growth of the world has been from all time toward greater and greater consciousness. We see this exemplified in the rise of the masses, the inauguration of democracies, the self-awareness of developing nations, in movements such as Women's Liberation, Children's Rights, etc. The world, then, is moving ever closer to consciousness, mind or spirit. Its direction is upward and toward the absolute and infinite, which each day blossoms more and more (that is, manifests itself in different movements, all tending toward awareness). The presence of Spirit or mind has always been there, but only now is it becoming more evident, uncovered, as it were, by Hegel's vision. That Spirit is universal, but shows itself only in a vague and particularized way, as yet. For example, in the eighteenth century, the "Spirit of '76" was a reality for Americans, helping produce a country which assumed increasing influence in the world. Its own expansionism could be explained in the nineteenth century by another instance of that spirit, now the "Spirit of Manifest Destiny." Today, the "Spirit of Freedom" is manifest in the changing attitudes tward the Third World. Working both for and against this aspect of Spirit, is an accompanying spirit of technology.

Is the Hegelian use of Spirit akin to a synonym for God? That is difficult to say, but indications are that this could be a very likely interpretation. If it is God, then God as Spirit *is not* (at least in any sense of fullness), but He is *becoming*. If such is the case, it appears that God is reality and reality is God, albeit with some important distinctions.

From this, and from Hegel's dialectical method, we see that God cannot be understood except in relation to the world, nor the world except in relationship to God. Each depends upon the other, in the way that consciousness needs an object, for consciousness is nothing, except that it be consciousness *of* something, i.e., the object; but it is also true that since an object is an object *for* consciousness, without the latter, there could be no object, either. Both need each other in a dialectical relationship. (This is similar to the fact that teacher and student both depend upon each other for meaning and development, or, as do, in Hegel's famous example, the Master and slave.)

As we have seen, Hegel is extremely difficult to understand, yet I think we are getting a glimpse into the emphasis and reality which he places on mind or spirit. In a more technical manner, what Hegel wants to show us is that reality is of whole cloth but dominated by mind. It consists of two elements which articulate and eventually merge into one. To understand his point about the dominance of mind (as well as its intersection with matter), let us ask the question, "Which is more important, the materials of a bridge or the mathematics which made it possible?" The mathematics, which is in the mind, can apply to all bridges and thus is universal. Yet each bridge is an individual bridge. As such, the *individual* bridge (matter) is a manifestation of the *universal* (mind). In this sense, the bridge is a concrete manifestation or objectification of subjective mind. The same would be true of an artist's painting or an author's book. Each is an instance of mind as concretized in this or that particular thing. Each is an idea become real and in so doing each becomes an object for consciousness. In a limited sense this is the way consciousness spreads itself out in space and nature. To sum up, while matter makes mind (spirit) concrete and particularized, mind (spirit) makes matter meaningful (intelligible). In this continuous dialectical interplay, there is an overall thrust and direction ever moving from nature to consciousness to self and Absolute Consciousness. What Hegel is suggesting is not that things are coming to be all in the mind, but that mind is coming to be all things and all things are coming to be mind. After various dualisms, Hegel has given us a monism again!

Influence

It is easy to see that, given the dialectical method, Hegel could have an appeal to those who wished to interpret religion on a purely natural basis. Indeed, in many respects, Hegel's thinking was the outcome and continuation of French Enlightenment thinking. We find there, naturalism, rationalism, and optimism, together with an unshakeable conviction in man's ability to discern the totality of his nature and that of reality. There was no need to appeal to a supernatural explanation; reason had access to all. Hegel's thought is really a philosophical anticipation of evolution, or put differently, evolution was to become a manifestation of Hegelian "mind."

One final word about Hegel's philosophy. When the individual is properly integrated within the universal there will be harmony. In human terms, men will enjoy a "happy consciousness" then only when each fully realizes his role within the society or community, i.e., the universal. The "unhappy consciousness" is such because it is aware of its separation and alienation from the community of mankind (universal). This sense of alienation was a point seized upon by Marx who saw it concretized in the 19th century sub-human conditions under which the worker existed. Workers were alienated from their very own labor; they may have produced the goods, but others took the profits from these.

Hegel's stress was on mind and reason, then, but waiting in the wings were many who opposed this tightly knit rationalism. They were to substitute for it the *mysterious* in philosophy, the *paradox* in religion and the *absurd* in the world. In a way, Hegel would have no objection to this for it fit the dialectical pattern of his thought. It is as if a mighty wave strikes the limits of the shore, only to bounce back to the ocean from whence it came, in the form of a strong undertow. The power of this itself is recollected and again thrust forward to the land.

Although Hegel influenced many, particularly in the area of theology, he generated few disciples. His idealistic philosophy, when ousted from Germany, was continued for a short time in England with men such as Bradley and Green. This is rather surprising, for the British temperament (and perhaps climate itself) has never proved favorable to idealism. For centuries it had been weaned almost exclusively on hard core empiricism and largely remains so to this day.

Here in America, Hegel's philosophical legacy was carried on by Josiah Royce. An Easterner who extensively travelled the West, he developed a highly interesting "philosophy of loyalty." In Italy, Hegelian ideas were disseminated by the philosopher-statesman, Benedetto Croce. In France, the sweep of Hegelian thought was influential on Henri Bergson and Pere Teilhard de Chardin. Both were outstanding thinkers, Bergson a Jew who served the cause of world peace and Chardin a Jesuit priest paleontologist.

Hegel's method, but not his philosophy, was taken over by Karl Marx. Marx claimed Hegel was right but only in reverse. It was Marx's intention to put Hegel standing upright. Thus it was that Marx took over the dialectical method of thesis, antithesis, and synthesis, but instead of making Spirit or *Mind* develop through history, Marx makes *matter* develop instead. Hence, while Hegel has an idealism, Marx possesses a materialism.

It may well be that few have heard of Georg Hegel, but there can be little doubt that his big ideas have left their mark on civilization.

GEORG HEGEL

Review Questions

1. In what way is Hegel a global thinker?
2. Does Hegel see reality as static or dynamic?
3. Give an example of the Hegelian dialectic, i.e., the way in which change occurs.
4. How does Hegel's logic differ from what one ordinarily understands logic to be?
5. What are some examples that argue to a continuing rise of consciousness?
6. Explain how two things such as master and slave, can only be understood in relation to each other.
7. Why is Hegel's philosophy called an absolute idealism?
8. Name two philosophers or thinkers who reflect or were influenced by Hegelian views.
9. Name one work written by Hegel.
10. If God is developing as Spirit, what are some logical implications which follow?

Special Thought Question

Does man in his private life reflect the rise and broadening of consciousness and sense of totality that might be seen in the world itself? How? In what stages?

BIBLIOGRAPHY

Primary Source: *Reason in History: A General Introduction to the Philosophy of History.* Tr. Robert S. Hartman (New York: Liberal Arts Press, 1953). (Discusses freedom, the State and an overview of history.)

Secondary Source: *The Philosophy of Hegel.* J. W. Finlay (New York: Collier Books, 1966). (An introduction to Hegel, but like all books dealing with Hegel, requires careful reading.)

10

SOREN KIERKEGAARD (1813–1855)

"A faith that celebrates its triumph is the most ridiculous thing conceivable." Philosophical Fragments

Religious Existentialism

The young have always had an idealistic bent and have prided themselves in being iconoclasts. Each has done his share of ranting against the Establishment. They seek rightly to discover for themselves new ways of living, new styles of dress and new insights into the nature of social institutions. They are looking for contemporary authors who share these views and reinforce them. Imagine the surprise of the young though, when they find a kindred spirit in a man who lived over one hundred years ago. And find him they have, for many are now reading Soren Kierkegaard. His books which he paid to have published are earning countless royalties for third parties today.

Psychologically, he was a most complex person; in terms of goals, he was quite simple. His task, as he put it, "was to reintroduce Christianity into Christendom."

By this he meant that the Church in Denmark (and elsewhere) was too bourgeois, too comfortable with its own official establishment as the State Church. Nearly everyone who was a Dane seemed to be automatically a Christian also. The ministers were state paid, took fishing vacations regularly and while preaching the triumph of Christ, neglected his passion. This hardly represented true Christianity, i.e., the life of struggle and suffering experienced by Jesus and his disciples. Christianity in the 19th century had become pharisaical, and Kierkegaard's satirical pen lashed out against this sham. As he tells us, the reality of Christianity had become an abstraction of "Christendom." It had gone full circle. Formerly in Christ's time fishermen disciples became "fishers of men." Today, "fishers of men" had once again become fishermen (a national pastime for Danes). Such a condition of religion mislead people into thinking that because they were institutionalized Christians, they were Christians in fact. Their worth lay in their collective life, not in their individual existence.

Kierkegaard's life was spent in calling attention to the necessity of each one of us recognizing oneself as an individual accountable for his own actions. This accountability is not to an abstract "Christendom" but must be given in "fear and trembling" before a demanding God. In laying stress on the individual (vs. Hegel's universal), Kierkegaard fathered what has come to be known as the movement of existentialism. It was a loose outlook on philosophical matters that took in such disparate thinkers such as Tolstoy, Nietzsche and Sartre. It stressed action, freedom, and commitment over speculative thought, emphasized concrete human existence over universal essences, and painted for us new categories of dread or *Angst*, despair, a sense of nothingness, the moment of truth and our "situationality" in the world. It asked not the abstract question, "What is man?" but the concrete one, "Who am I?"

To understand Kierkegaard and his work, we must try to understand his life, for his task came out of his life experiences. As the great Johann Gottlieb Fichte once wrote, "What kind of philosophy one may choose depends on what kind of human being one is; for a philosophical system is ensouled by the soul of the human being who has it."

Early Life

Soren Kierkegaard was born in Copenhagen, Denmark in 1813. He was the last of seven children, the son of his father's second wife. There seems to have been a hint of scandal suggesting that the latter was a "shotgun" marriage. At any rate, we find virtually no reference of Kierkegaard to his mother and nearly a total identity of himself with his father. The father, Michael, was 57 years old when Soren was born and from the very beginning, the son took on the troubles of his father. Melancholy all his life, Soren tells us he was "born an old man." The deep sense of guilt which long has been traditional with Lutheranism left its mark on the father and through the father upon the son. Both took to heart Luther's preaching that "Before God, I am always in the wrong!" The guilt complex of the father was especially deep rooted. As an impoverished youth, he had cursed God for his lot in life, tending sheep on the cold plains of Jutland. Since that time, the father became financially well to do and paradoxically regarded this as God's reminder-punishment to him, rather than a blessing as seen by the world. The irony felt by the old man left its mark on Soren, who in his college days, wrote his dissertation on the concept of irony.

Soren was a cripple with a deformed back due probably to injuries suffered in a fall from a tree. He walked with a noticeable limp and was generally in poor health. Possibly for these reasons, Michael was particularly attached to him. Frequently, Soren's father would take long walks with him in the garden. There he would tell the youngster about the world (for Michael was well traveled) and even discuss philosophy.

For some years, Soren studied for the ministry. One of his brothers already was a Bishop and the Primate of Denmark, Bishop Mynster, was a friend of the family. The established church, of course, was the Danish Evangelical Lutheran Church. Soren studied both in Copenhagen and in Berlin, but despite his desire to be a minister saw his calling from another direction. It was a decision reached in pathos and anguish and required him to break off his marriage engagement with a young lady, Regine Olsen. This proved to be a bit scandalous, but Soren shouldered its burden completely by himself. At one time he was on the verge of suicide, but gradually he came to see his life's task. Posing as a dilettante to the public, he became a deep and serious critic of the Church, much as Socrates was the gadfly to the self satisfied Athenians. Socrates' motto of "Know thyself" inscribed on the Delphic Temple was interpreted by Kierkegaard as "Choose yourself!" Recognize yourself as an individual with all the responsibilities and implications that attend this. In every endeavor one must illustrate a "purity of heart," or authenticity, as it came to be known. Kierkegaard set himself up as the "loyal opposition" to the Church, which he envisioned as leading its members away from what it was to be a Christian, by encouraging persons to believe they were such already. Just as the Socratic wisdom of Plato's mentor emphasized that to seek truth we first must be aware of our own ignorance, so to become a Christian, one must first realize that one is not a Christian.

Either Philosophy or Religion

As we have read earlier, one of the leading intellectual influences in nineteenth-century Germany was the philosophy of Georg Hegel. It was a philosophy which explained everything in a rationalistic manner. Nothing was left unexplained. Everything fit into the "System," as Kierkegaard ironically dubbed Hegel's philosophy.

Had Hegel's philosophy kept to the realm of philosophy, Kierkegaard would not have registered a protest. As Kierkegaard saw it, however, Hegel's philosophy began to absorb religion. Now, as one might expect, the small country of Denmark was heavily influenced by German "Kultur." Philosophy was no exception. Many of the theologicans and ministers in the Danish Church were sent to Germany and trained in Hegelian philosophy.

Now it was Kierkegaard's contention that the Church hierarchy was being deceived by philosophy. What was worse, they were deceiving the congregations. As Kierkegaard viewed it, the ministers were no longer ministers, but philosophers and professors. They were not preaching salvation and suffering to the people; quite the contrary, they were offering philosophical speculation in its stead. The very ministers of God's words had themselves forgotten Luther's reminder that, "Faith is a function of the Spirit, Reason is a function of the Flesh."

In Hegelian philosophy, things were becoming more and more perfect. Victory, like prosperity, was just around the corner. Taking their cue from this, the ministers were offering a Church Triumphant, instead of a Church Militant to the people. Kierkegaard put it this way, "Nowadays, one is more likely to hear a sermon end with a 'Hurrah!' rather then with an 'Amen.'" He could not remain silent on these matters. Toward the Church, he assumed an increasingly critical stance, privately and in public. His original writings such as *The Concept of Dread*, were published under a pseudonym. Later, he published them under his editorship and eventually under his authorship. Although he wrote various *Discourses on Love*, beautiful and inspiring pieces of literature, most of his works were polemical. Examples would be *Philosophical Fragments* and the articles published in *Attack Upon Christendom*. His sharp-tongued barbs against the Church he felt were necessary because, "Now, one goes to the theatre to be edified and the Church to be entertained." But he did not limit his polemic to the Church. He became involved with the media of his time, particularly a newspaper named *The Corsair*. He thrusted and parried with the intellectuals of the Danish coffee houses. Back in his room, he confided to his *Journals* that things were proceeding well. His critiques became more strident, when in the late 1840's he experienced an insight that God not only forgave his sins, but He *forgot* them as well.

Attack Upon Philosophy

Kierkegaard complained that one can get so involved in abstraction, as to forget about reality. The philosopher can build beautiful dream castles from an ivory tower, and yet live in a dog house beside it. To illustrate how a scholar could lose touch with reality, Kierkegaard tells us of the man who pored over a manuscript for two days, trying to understand why a period should appear at the end of a particular word. It made no sense, but there it was. Well, to make a long story short, his housekeeper was looking over his shoulder and saw the dot and simply whisked it away—for it was a speck of dust. She had not lost her touch with reality, but the scholar had.

Acting as critic, Soren kept insisting that the true Christian life is not one of philosophy, but of religion, not one of comfort, but one of suffering. To go forward in Christianity, one must go backward to Christ. Hence, for Kierkegaard, unlike the views of Hegelian theologians, Christianity was more perfect in the past than in the present or future. It was a primitive Christianity which he sought. As Kierkegaard saw it, his task was to substitute the subjective for objective, the concrete for the abstract, the individual for the universal, and existence for essence.

Kierkegaard did not refute Hegel on the battlefield of philosophy. This would have been quite ineffective. Instead, he laughed it to scorn. He exaggerated it to reveal its utter folly when brought into Christianity. He did this by calling attention to the fact that "the most injurious thing to digestion is constant reflection on digestion." In our own day, we might ask apropos this insight, "How many marriages and how many vocations have been wrecked by such agonizing examinations questioning whether or not one has a good marriage, a true vocation, etc." The thing is not to reflect but to live out the situation. Praxis, not theoria is proper to such situations.

The call of the Christian is not to action stifling speculation, but commitment to Christ. The Christian knows he must make an "either/or" decision, if he recalls what Christ said about those who are lukewarm. Says Kierkegaard, "If you want to sew, knot the thread!" Make a commitment! With such a devastating attack, he dethroned idealistic philosophy so completely, that to this day, few traces remain.

A Call to the Individual

Kierkegaard wanted to wake up the people in order to have them face the question of "Who Am I?" and "Why Am I Here?" But the difficulty confronting him was how to attack the masses—the masses, itself an abstraction, for there are only individuals. Yet he found a way, as he tells us in his diary. He would make the masses strike him! This he did! Extremely polemical, as mentioned before, he attacked the intellectuals of the day, Henrik Ibsen and Hans Christian Andersen. (They in turn attacked him through caricatures in their writings.) He attacked the Danish Primate and his successor. The means proved to be most effective to the success of his cause, but they worked to his own personal detriment as well.

In awakening the people to their responsibilities of being Christians, Kierkegaard appealed not to abstract categories which have little or no meaning. Rather his appeal was to the existential categories of guilt, dread, despair, anguish, fear, etc. Possessed of keen psychological insights, he explored these concepts of their depths (and in so doing has influenced depth psychology and existential psychology in our own time). For example, fear is different than dread or *Angst*. Fear always is of something specific, such as fear of enclosed places, fear of heights, etc. These fears can be cast aside by avoiding the situation which produces them. Dread, however, has nothingness for its object—the nothingness of the human condition, the "vent" described so well by Sartre.

All have experienced the anguish and the guilt of sin and Kierkegaard uses these common bonds to make us aware of what it means to bear witness to the truth, not by way of a judgement of speculative assent, but by way of an existential life. There is, after all, a great difference between knowing the truths of natural science, of the fact that the earth is round, that the sun is ninety-three million miles away, etc., and the seeking of the Truth (spelled with a capital "T") to be found in Christ, Who is the Truth! It is of this latter Truth that he observes, "Truth is a snare; you do not catch it. It catches you!" We are to love the truth, not just know it. We are to live in truth, much as St. Augustine advises; it is only thereby that we become true to ourselves and to God.

Three Stages of Existence

If we look at ourselves, muses Kierkegaard, we can see that existence can be typified by three different stages. There is the *Aesthetic Stage* of life where one lives the character of an automaton, never making a real decision. Characterized by the Don Juan or Faust, it is a life of utter sensuousness or hedonism. It may also be more insidious when it is typified by the Professor who lives in a world of abstraction, thinking that this is reality. The characteristic of this stage is *pleasure* and all is subordinated to it. Here, a person's end lies wholly in externals. Basically, the individual in the aesthetic stage of existence lives the life of a robber, taking everything out of life, but putting nothing back into it. It is a life in which we find that the busier we are, the more bored we become. It has no real seriousness about it. Existentially, it has no purpose. It is a life of hidden despair, yet its participant is not aware even of this. Such awareness must be won to confront this stage and to be able to move to a higher level of existence.

On the other hand, there is the *Ethical Stage* of existence, in which a kind of universal morality prevails. It is a stage in which the average person discovers himself, a stage in which one acts out of the motivation of fear of punishment or hope for reward. Typified by the monk, the category governing this level of life is that of *duty*. (We might add that Kierkegaard was very sympatico with the life of the monk celibate. Nonetheless, it did not escape his criticism, for he felt that it contained its own brand of ostentation. The robes of the monk signified *to the world* who he was, the sacrifices he was making, etc. The life lacked what was an essential aspect of Christianity, hidden inwardness. He reminded Kierkegaard of an Alderman, who announced his position through his robes and medals.)

But now we come to the highest level of human existence. This level is the *Religious Stage* and it is aptly revealed by the martyr. Actions are done out of love for God. Here man sees himself as an individual before God, in what is almost a kind of private religion. Here, a definitely personal relationship is established. There is a hint of mysticism to be seen, but it is a mysticism available to all men. In order to attain this stage, we must come to know the importance of recognizing the "paradox." A paradox might be described as "a seeming absurdity grounded on truth."

For example, in earlier stages of existence, the paradox manifests itself in various stumbling blocks which at first appear to hinder faith. These offend us and require us to sit up and take notice. In the religious stage we welcome the paradox and set reason aside to become lost in faith.

What are some of the paradoxes of which Kierkegaard writes? He is partial to the *Old Testament*, but draws upon the *New Testament* as well. The Test of Abraham when God asked him to sacrifice his son Isaac was one. Another was the fact that Moses who led the Chosen People to the Promised Land, himself was not allowed to enter. Then too the inheritance story of Jacob and Esau, the youngest getting the legacy and the story of Joseph and his brothers who wished to get rid of him, ending up in Joseph ruling the others—all are paradoxes and show God's penchant for the unexpected. This aspect of a "Trickster God" had great appeal to Soren who felt his own life mirrored these. The supreme paradox, of course, was the notion of the God-Man, Jesus Christ. One could not dream up a more insane combination, he says, and yet it is a decisive fact of faith. The list goes on to include that we must use time to enter eternity, and that if we are sure we have faith, we can be sure we don't have it. We must live somewhere between presumption and despair and rely entirely on God. No wonder it is that Kierkegaard described Christianity as Paradox Religion! Given such paradoxes, to be given faith, we must take a leap (*Sprung*). With it, we leave the world of reason and enter God's world.

For Kierkegaard, then, the true Christian is the one who is striving toward Christianity, he is the one who is *becoming* a Christian, but *is not* one. Man must raise the crisis of his existence, but by himself he cannot resolve it. For this, faith and grace are necessary. He must reject freedom to gain it again in faith. He must reject the certainties of reason to gain much more certainty in faith. He must welcome the paradox to overcome it.

In the final analysis, Kierkegaard's anti-institutionalism with respect to the Church pushed him in the direction of a kind of *laissez faire* Christianity, the kind that stressed the eventual standing before God by the individual, who alone is responsible for his actions. A last final absurdity awaited Soren. On the day he died in 1855, the last dollar of his inheritance ran out!

Kierkegaard Today

The influence of Kierkegaard is a strong one and not only in Protestant circles, among such men as Paul Tillich, Emil Brunner, Karl Barth and Reinhold Nierbuhr. It is also strong in the Jewish tradition of Martin Buber and in the Catholic, Gabriel Marcel. It is present also in the atheist, Jean-Paul Sartre.

Kierkegaard's appraisal of the Lutheran and Roman Catholic Church may well have signaled the movement toward ecumenism. Equally he berated both Luther and the Papacy, but suggested that if the Reformation began as a protest to Catholic corruption, now that much of the corruption was wiped out, they no longer should remain apart. It was a simple idea, but one that has profound consequences.

It may be true that as one scholar puts it, the existentialism of Kierkegaard died with Kierkegaard; but it is also true that he has helped contemporary man phrase for himself the important existential question of life. In our age of bureaucracy and of faceless men, it is more important than ever to find our own identity as individuals. In this endeavor, the spirit of Soren Kierkegaard still lives in us all.

SOREN KIERKEGAARD

Review Questions

1. In what way can Kierkegaard be regarded as the "father" of contemporary existentialism?
2. What did Kierkegaard mean by "paradox?" Give two examples of paradoxes as Kierkegaard saw them in his own life.
3. What dominant philosophy of the time did Kierkegaard react against and why?
4. How did Kierkegaard hope to make the masses aware of their condition?
5. What is the difference between truth and Truth?
6. Explain: One cannot start becoming a Christian until one is aware that one is not a Christian.
7. What are the three stages of existence?
8. By himself, man can move from the first to the second stage of existence, but not from the second to the third. Why?
9. Name the two men influenced by Kierkegaard or two movements today which might be traceable to his influence.
10. Explain: If I am sure I have faith, I can be sure I don't have it.

Special Thought Question

Can one follow Kierkegaard's ideas and still adhere to institutional religion?

BIBLIOGRAPHY

Primary Source: *A Kierkegaard Anthology.* Ed. R. Bretall (New York: Modern Library, 1946). (A selection of texts from a broad spectrum of Kierkegaard's writings.)

Secondary Source: *Six Existentialist Thinkers.* H. J. Blackham (New York: Harper Torchbooks, 1959). (A very readable summary of Kierkegaard, Marcel, Sartre, and three others in this tradition.)

11
KARL MARX (1818–1883)

"The history of all hitherto existing society is the history of class struggles." Communist Manifesto

Dialectical Materialism

As we know, the charge is often made against philosophers that they are concerned only with the abstract, that they know nothing of the practical order and that they even view the practical order with disdain. It is also alleged that the ideas of philosophers have little significance when it comes to the way we live our lives.

Such views, of course, are erroneous; the charges are unfounded, for in the final analysis, whether we like it or not, the world is run by ideas.

Now we know that every revolution has its own philosophy but for the first time we are to meet up with a philosophy that spawns its own revolution. It was a philosophy which centered around economic theory but always appealed to praxis, that is, to practical and pragmatic action. The philosophy to which we refer is the philosophy of Karl Heinrich Marx. Describing it he says, "philosophy is its own time apprehended in thought." Let us take a look at the times of Karl Marx to understand the philosophy he offers. Throughout this study, though, we must be careful not to identify it with any particular system of government, or even current political ideology, i.e., a rationalization of the established order. Many have used and equally many have abused his notions. Let us study them as objectively as we can, as befits philosophers examining the works of colleagues.

Biographical Notes

Karl Marx was born in Trier, Prussia (present day western Germany) in 1818. His grandfather was a Jewish Rabbi and his father a Jewish lawyer.

Apparently for political reasons the family converted to Lutheranism when Karl was six years old. It was a formality rather than a matter of conviction, for there was virtually no practice of the religion by the family.

At first it appeared that like his father, Karl Marx would go into the legal profession. However, Marx's interest in law was short-lived. He became more enamoured with history and especially with philosophy. He studied at Bonn, Berlin and eventually won his doctorate at the University of Jena. He wrote his dissertation on the materialism of two ancient philosophers, who were termed atomists, for whom all reality was explained by small particles of matter.

Marx's life was a stormy one marked by many frustrations. He edited a small paper for a time in Germany, but the paper was suppressed. Moving to Paris, he edited a Yearbook, but was expelled from France at the request of the Prussian government. His views all the while crystalizing during this tumultous period, in 1845 in his *Theses on Feurbach*, he declares that absolute truth can never be one restricted to theory. It must be practical. "The reality and power of thought must be shown in practice by *both* explaining and changing the world." The truly important thing is not to understand history (to which Hegel devoted his chief attention), but to change it. After a short stay in Brussels, Belgium, Marx returned to Germany during the revolution of 1848. Here, he organized (unfruitfully) the German Socialist Party and again edited a paper. It, too, went under in 1849 and Marx moved to London.

By now, Marx had a wife and four children and supported himself and his family by eking out a living from writing articles for the *New York Tribune*. Tragedy struck the family during this time, for three of his children died, his wife suffered a breakdown and Marx himself became afflicted with various physical ailments.

Fortunately for Marx, a friend whom he met in earlier editorial days, Friedrich Engels, came to his assistance from time to time. Engels was a wealthy manufacturer from Manchester, England, who in earlier days had collaborated with Marx in writing the *Communist Manifesto*, published in 1848. (The ideas of both men are so similar that it is difficult to separate their positions. Consequently, the overview to follow is representative of the combination, rather than Marx alone.)

Marx helped found the *First Socialist Internationale* in London in 1864, but it persevered for only a few years. Later a *Second Internationale* was formed and eventually a *Third* Internationale. The present one in Russia replaced it. Marx came out with his most famous work, *Das Kapital*, in 1867, a publication in which he attempts to formulate the economic laws which govern and move modern society. The second and third volumes of this work were edited by Engels and published after the death of Marx which occurred in 1883.

Although sometimes disputed, I believe Marx always considered himself a philosopher, rather than simply economic theoretician. We can see this by his following reflective comments which are clearly applicable to himself.

> Philosophers do not grow like mushrooms, out of the earth; they are the outgrowth of their period, their nation, whose most subtle delicate and invisible juice abounds in the philosophical ideas. The same spirit that constructs the philosophical system in the mind of the philosopher builds the railways with the hands of the trade. Philosophy does not reside outside the world just as the mind does not reside outside man, just because it is not located in his belly.

Marx's Intellectual Heritage

During his lifetime, Marx drew heavily from his contemporaries. As we recall, the most important philosopher was Hegel, who Marx studied intensely. Followers of Hegel split into two camps, Right Wing Hegelians and Left Wing Hegelians. It was the latter whom Marx drew upon, philosophers such as David Strauss and Bruno Bauer. (Both looked upon religion as myth.) Another Left Hegelian was Ludwig Feuerbach, a former idealist, turned materialist. Feuerback also attacked religion, asserting that God is simply a projection by man of himself considered as an ideal. According to Feuerbach, true theology is really anthropology. By this he meant that since man produces God, a study of God in the final analysis was a study of man. (Freud was to hold a similar position, later.) This projection of man by man (in the form of God) produced fragmentation or alienation, for it separated man from his own true nature.

Furthermore, according to Feuerbach, "Man is what he eats." In a sense, man creates himself, since he produces his food. Through better food, such as more protein, etc., he alters and improves his physical and mental condition. Since he does this through work, it is his work that renders his more and more human, moving him ever higher up in the evolutionary scale. Man, then, is a worker-man. To understand man, one must understand the nature of work.

A few remarks on historical attitudes toward "work" may be in order, for work was seen differently in different cultures. It always distinguished man from the brute animal, and men wondered why work was peculiar to them. For the ancient Hebrews, although each man should teach his son a trade, work essentially was a punishment for sin. Adam and Eve were cast out of a non-work Paradise and forced to live by labor and the "sweat of their brow." It was a "hard necessity." By and large, the Greeks thought work was fitting only for slaves, not free men. Romans looked upon agriculture and commerce as the only kind of worth-while work, and early Christians accepted it as a way to distract one from the sinful enticements of the world. "An idle mind is the devil's workshop." Work came to have an intrinsic and universal value first in the thought of Luther. Calvin advocated it and the profits which derived from it were a possible sign of God's favor and election. (Cf. in general the "Protestant Work Ethic.) Others viewed work as a way to restore virtue, i.e., the punishment for criminals being so many months at hard labor. For many in the Russian culture, such as Tolstoy, work was as natural to man as breathing.

Given this background, let us return to Marx. Any economic system that robs the worker-man of the fruits of his labor, alienates man by separating man from what is rightfully his and needed by him to perfect himself. (This makes intelligible the Marxist charge today that a capitalist society which is committed practically to a five per cent unemployment rate for its members is immoral. It is immoral because it does not permit this five per cent to become human by means of their work. If they cannot be workers they are non-persons.)

Marx Comes Into His Own

Marx listened well to such thinkers and incorporated their criticism into his own. He utilized the dialectical method of Hegel, but applied it to matter, rather than to mind. He accused Hegel of standing on his head and living in a world of upside downness, a *verkehrte Welt*. For Marx it is not mind that unfolds (Hegel) but matter, though eventually it produces mind or consciousness as its highest manifestation. Absolute Spirit (Hegel) becomes nothing more than the eruption of impersonal material energy, a throwback to Marx's writings on the Atomists in his dissertation.

While Hegel's philosophy had been known as a dialectical idealism, Marx's thought would be termed dialectical materialism. However, Marx himself had always been interested in human history and he saw its development as dependent upon certain economic, social and material factors or laws. Thus Marx's interest lay more in *historical materialism*, rather than primarily in *dialectical materialism*.

Marx's Analysis of History

Marx sought to show that there are certain economic and political factors which determine man's development, rather than man determining these factors.

Perhaps an example will illustrate this. In our own country, the Sioux Indians were among the greatest and most feared warriors. They were good at war! One reason was because they eventually took residence in the high plains of the Dakotas, where buffalo were plentiful. One buffalo could feed many more people than the rabbits, deer and fish of the woodlands Indians. This, together with the introduction of the horse, gave them leisure time for doing something other than scrounging for food. They turned to war for honor and booty and the more frequently they practiced it, the more adept they became at it. The woodland Indians, having no time for war, suffered from lack of practice and so dared not challenge the power of the Sioux. In short, the Sioux were the "haves," the woodland Indians, the "have nots."

For Marx, then, history determined man, rather than man determines history. What is important in history then is its economic base, not its culture superstructure. Change that base and one changes history and therefore man. But we must remember, argues Marx, that it is not the individual who exerts this change for the better, i.e., the cult of personality so roundly condemned in Marxist states today. Rather it is the masses which constitute that driving force, for man is unique as a "species-being," that is, an individual who realizes that he is part of a social fabric in which and from which he achieves his identity. (We can now see that the masses have come to replace the role of Spirit as outlined in Hegelian philosophy.) For Marx, then, man's essence is nothing abstract, but the concrete ensemble of his social relations. To improve man, one must improve these social relations, for man has no nature, only a history.

As Marx saw it, all history is a documentation and dynamic development of the class struggle in which the underdog has eventually won out. In every battle between the conservative and the liberal, the conservative has lost. Whether the struggle was between the Greek slave and his master, the feudal serf and his baron, or between the employee and the employer, the result for Marx would be inevitable, namely, the eventual overcoming of the privileged by the underprivileged.

The worker class Marx called the *proletariat;* the capitalist was termed the *bourgeoisie.* In order to speed up the inevitable victory of the proletariat over the bourgeoisie, Marx issued his famous call to arms, "Workers of the world unite!"

The Problem With Capitalism

Marx, living as he did in the backwash of one hundred years of the Industrial Revolution, witnessed that the worker was in a terrible plight. One has only to read Charles Dickens and the history of coal mining, mills, etc., to get a vivid picture of the squalor and misery that prevailed among the workers. Their social condition gave rise to an impossible sense of *alienation*. It is an issue central to Marx's humanism. His classic description follows:

Alienation is apparent not only in the fact that my means of life belong to someone else, that my desires are the unattainable possession of someone else, but that everything is something different from itself, that my activity is something else, and finally . . . that an inhuman power rules over everything.

A concrete example of the above, says Marx, is the fact that in his time one was "at home" only in one's animal activities, such as sex and eating, while in one's human activities, work, one was miserable. It was an upside down world! The basic evils responsible for these lamentable conditions were private property and economic laws. These were backed up by the state which was favorable to the capitalist but disadvantageous to the worker.

Marx theorized that originally in the "state of nature" there were no class divisions. There was no private property. However the strong put down the weak and made the latter subservient. Enforcing their own wishes to suppress others, they *invented* the State. In addition to this, there was the factor of organized religion which Marx regarded as "an opiate of the people"; for it tended to keep them from revolting, through appeal to rewards of an afterlife. In short, the State and Religion were inventions of the well to do, specifically designed to keep the worker in his place. As man-formed, they should be at his service. Instead man only bows down before these.

In giving further sophistication to his theories, Marx elaborated on the defects of capitalism. Its so called "law of supply and demand," if a law at all, was a law of the jungle, not of societal and civilized man. In capitalism is an inherent sleight of hand trick constantly played upon the worker. Employing it is how capitalists get richer and workers become poorer.

We can distinguish several factors at play here. One might be termed the means or *forces of production* and these would be constituted by the tools, technics and labor of the day. The other factor can be termed the *relations of production* and what Marx appears to mean here, is the attitude, agreements and general relationships between employees and employer.

Nineteenth century industry increased productivity by new methods and machinery but not wages. Since the worker produced more, not as many were needed. The scarcity of jobs forced workers to work for less wages in order to get work. Looking at Marx's age, much of this social criticism was true, and is still true in some underdeveloped countries, but no longer on such a large scale as before. At the same time we must recognize that the capitalism against which Marx ranted was the *laissez-faire* capitalism which frankly is no longer around, at least in developed countries.

In Marx's analysis, the laws of society are such that the relations of production must give way to new relations. Yet the capitalist refuses to concede anything; refuses to relinguish the upper hand in any of these matters. Hence, the capitalist is responsible for the resulting class struggle which will eventually result in his downfall. According to Marx, the capitalist has given up certain strengths only begrudgingly and only at the forcing of his hand by the worker. To enforce further demands, the worker therefore must collectivize. Thus the worker should create unions, boycotts, and various economic pressures to obtain what is rightfully his, i.e., the value of his work. Continuing, Marx viewed capitalism as having nearly reached the end of its road, for there were certain inherent difficulties in it which could not be overcome. Examples seen in Marx's time were chronic unemployment and poverty amidst plenty.

With the many evil effects being felt by the Industrial Revolution, Marx thought that the machine aggravated the opposition of worker to employer and created an alienating "division of labor." His call was for eventual expropriation of all capitalists. However, it was not imperative that this be accomplished by overt and violent means.

Marx's Corrective

How did Marx propose to correct the situation? Well, there are many ways he suggested. Because he thought that a capitalistic system would result in the progressive pauperization of the masses in which the rich would become richer and the poor become poorer, Marx suggested a new way to determine the value of the product manufactured or discovered. In short, Marx asked how we can determine the worth of a product. By a free market? No, Marx suggests this would be unjust. The only way it appears that all products could be compared as to value, would be to discover some common element found in all. That common element was the amount of work put into the item. Thus, the value of a product should not be determined by supply and demand, but on the basis of the amount of work put into it. In such a system, only the worker can give value, which is a kind of truth. Hence, in certain Marxist states, even the administrators of a government do some work each week. This is also why there is the appeal to women to be workers, so that additional value can be created.

Once again then, for Marx, it was time to change the relations of production, by controlling the means of production. That is, by having the state control factories and the general means over producing capital goods. In this fashion, there would gradually develop the "dictatorship of the proletariat," the worker-state. In this process socialism would appear first with its motto "To each according to his work performed." Next would appear communism with its motto, "From each according to his ability, to each according to his needs." With this, the state would wither away and a classless society would be present. This milennium is the goal of the Marxists. N.B. "Marxist" in this context refers to those who use Marx's ideas as the basis of their own ideology, but who often revise it, sometimes in such a way as to be unrecognizable to Marx himself, were he alive today.

While Marxism has undergone many refinements since the nineteenth century, its principles remain essentially the same. Man, though a product of matter has achieved consciousness and is now in a position to direct his own destiny—a destiny which is collective, not individual. Through his consciousness, he knows the world and acts within it. His knowledge constitutes a copy of things as they are. Seeing these and garnering "insight into necessity," i.e., the laws that govern progress, man can be regarded as free, for this is the nature of freedom in the concrete.

Conclusion

Some of the criticisms made by Marx were quite valid in the nineteenth century when industrialization was in its infancy. Children were working 12 hours a day in mines and mills. The worker was often held to a starvation wage while many employers became immensely wealthy. Fortunately, the laissez-faire capitalism of the nineteenth century is no longer prevalent in our own country and Marxist criticism is shallow and empty here. Workers do share in the fruits of their labor. Profit sharing plans, bonuses, unions, social legislation, etc. have rendered obsolete the observations of Marx with reference to capitalism.

Unfortunately, however, the situation in some Third World countries of South America and Africa closely parallel the laissez-faire capitalism of the nineteenth century in which Marx lived. There we see that his ideas are very much alive, especially as reinforced by thinkers such as Lenin. Many of these countries look to the giant leaps of *Russia* and *China* and feel they may do the same. Modifications of Marxism indeed are working hand in hand with religion-oriented peoples in these countries, for both claim a common interest in humanism. This "marriage of convenience" may be only temporary, however, when one considers the long range outlook of Marxism and its understanding of historical development.

KARL MARX

Review Questions

1. Give some bits of Marx's biography.
2. What did Marx mean when he said what is important is not so much to understand history as to change it?
3. What was the relationship of Engels to Marx?
4. Explain: Marx thought Hegel was correct but his philosophy was upside down.
5. How does man produce himself through his work?
6. Give an example of Hegel's dialectic as employed by Marx.
7. Does society change the individual or the individual change society according to Marx?
8. What is the basis for Marx's opposition to religion?
9. Distinguish the relations of production from the forces of production?
10. What would Marx use as the criterion for the value of any product?

Special Thought Question

Is Marxism itself a form of religion? Explain.

BIBLIOGRAPHY

Primary Source: *Basic Writings on Politics and Philosophy.* Ed. Lewis Feuer (New York: Doubleday & Co., 1959). (Contains the most important works of Marx and Engels.)

Secondary Source: *The Life and Teaching of Karl Marx.* John Lewis (New York: International Publishing Co., c. 1965). (Good biography and overview of principal positions of Marx.)

12
FRIEDRICH WILHELM NIETZSCHE (1844–1900)

"What is falling, should also be pushed." So Spoke Zarathustra

Recently, a cartoon showed some graffiti on a wall which read, "God is dead! (Signed) Nietzsche." The next day the same sign was crossed out and in its place was, "Nietzsche is dead! (Signed) God." Pretty well, this is about the extent of the average person's knowledge of Nietzsche. Yet Nietzsche was a philosopher to be reckoned with, a wild man to be sure, but one who like a prophet of old, served as critic of his own and of our time as well.

In Shakespeare's *Hamlet* the young Dane muses over his life in which he had been accused of madness by some. Yet old Polonius, upon listening to the ranting remarks murmurs, "If this be madness, methinks there is method in it." We might say the same of Nietzsche, who spent the last decade of his life insane. He was a madman, a poet, a visionary and a prophet, but in his madness, there was meaning, deep meaning, for he raised questions which most of us would prefer to ignore or "sweep under the rug." In many ways, the issues he addressed are more germane today than even in his own era. Let's take a look, then, at his times and our times and face squarely and honestly the criticism he raises—if we dare!

Life and Times

Friedrich Nietzsche was born in 1844. From that time, until his death in 1900, Europe was astir with romanticism with its stress on the glorification of freedom. There are no constraints on the mind in thinking new thoughts and for humans seeking new endeavors. German idealism (which some read as subjectivism) also abounded. Strong forces were at work, nearly all of them romantically depicting some form of power. The period in Germany was known as that of *Sturm und Drang* (storm and stress). It was the age of the Iron Chancellor, Otto von Bismarck from whom the capitol city in North Dakota was derived. His rule was characterized as *Blut und Isen* (Blood and Iron), and it found bitter and brutal expression in the Franco-Prussian War.

In art, the Swiss painter Arnold Bocklin, was idolized by Germans for his powerful themes of romanticism, though always depicted in a "harsh" manner. In music, the kettle drums of Wagnerian opera sounded the fury of the times. His *Love and Death* with its ever rising crescendos and the *Ride of the Valkyries* praising slain Nordic heroes gave a visible chill and thrill to all who heard his music. His Brunhilde and Siegfried represented Germanic ideas.

Another expression of this romanticism was King Ludwig's building of the Bavarian castle Neuschwanstein, the model for Disneyworld. The inside walls of the castle are painted with scenes from different Wagnerian operas. (Mad Ludwig he was called, for he ran his principality into debt. Nonetheless, the twentieth-century tourist trade has vindicated his "madness" by filling its coffers far and beyond the original costs of the castle.)

Philosophically, we see in the background of Nietzsche's times the influence of Kant, with his claim for our inability to know reality "as it is in itself." Coupled with this is the construction of reality through its interface with Hegelian *Geist* (mind). Lastly, the spectre of Marxism was making its own intellectual impact with its emphasis on the collective. This then is the setting into which Friedrich Nietzsche was born and reared, the son of a Lutheran paster in Rocken, Prussian Saxony.

Frederich's father died in the boy's youth and he was brought up in an extremely feminine, not to say, prissy, environment. Throughout his life Nietzsche was plagued with headaches and pains of every sort and description. Some perhaps could be attributed to hypochrondia. In many ways a Freudian would have a field day in psychoanalyzing the basis of Nietzsche's call for a will to power. In the last analysis, the German's writings are essentially biographical as Nietzsche himself hints. His projection of the overman appears to be his ideal self, much as Aristotle's god as "Self-Thinking-Thought" mirrored his ideal man.

For many years Nietzsche was a devoted friend of Wagner, especially the struggling Wagner. Perhaps Nietzsche saw in such striving a manifestation of his own call for a will to power. When Wagner did achieve acclaim and recognition, the friendship dissolved, possibly because Wagner's struggle for fame was over now and he could rest on his laurels—a life style to which Nietzsche was vehemently opposed. In fact the year 1888 saw Nietzsche launch a vicious attack on Wagner. The two never were reconciled again.

There is no question but that Nietzsche was a gifted individual. His mind never engaged in idling but always raced. In some ways his body could not keep up with this delicately tuned engine. Recognition of his talent was acknowledged publicly with his appointment to a Chair in Philology (language speciality) at the Swiss University of Basle in 1869. This appointment came *despite* the fact that he had not yet earned a doctorate, almost a necessary condition for such a post. He served for a time in the German Army, but was injured in a fall from his horse. By the time he recovered, his conscription period was up. It was just as well for he really could not take its rigors and this allowed him to return to a more sedentary academic life.

During several years spent as a student at Leipzig, he came to read the writings of Schopenhauer (1788–1860) and these lifted the veil from his eyes and gave him direction for his own philosophical outlook. Schopenhauer, who was familiar with Eastern thought (particularly Buddhism and its views on evil) couldn't reconcile the beauty of nature and the misery of human life. His own life was witness to this misery and he freely projected it everywhere he could, even to the point of being a woman-hater. Looking for the source of this misery in existence, he concluded that the reason for all *Weltschmerz* (universal pain) is man's own will, his own striving. We must negate this striving, this force of will and accept what is. Out of this conviction came his book, *The World as Will and Ideas*, and it provided the entree to Nietzsche's thought.

Seizing upon will as fundamental and irreducible, instead of negating life as did Schopenhauer, Nietzsche uses it to *affirm* life in face of all chaos and obstacles. What matter is it if we can't know reality (Kant)?; for practical purposes this is mere chaos anyway. We can make our mark upon the world—more correctly, we can create the reality we call world through a sheer imposition of power, will power, *the will to power!*

Nietzsche recalled how once in his childhood he watched with fascination as a farmer slit the throats of two goats during the time of a thunderstorm replete with lightning flashes. At the time, he was puzzled at his own exhilaration of this raw exercise of power. It was all the more so because he himself was a "gentle and sensitive" soul. Now he saw that this exuberant and exhilarating will to power itself was the very apex of reality and the goal of all who would be men. Like William James and Teddy Roosevelt, themselves nineteenth century figures, he urged the strenuous life as breeding this inner and outer strength. He praised war, saying, "Ye shall love peace as a means to new wars. And the short peace more than the long . . ." Again, "Man shall be trained for war, and women for the recreation of the warrior." We should seek to command, for "To Command is harder than to obey." At all times he extolled the dangerous and risk-taking life over that of the hedonistic one of sheer comfort. Yet these writings of Nietzsche easily can be misunderstood and especially can they be taken out of context. Thus, we will examine them in detail later in this chapter.

Although a thorough-going scholar, Nietzsche was not content with such a life. It struck him as dry, tedious and even boring. He longed to be the man of whom he wrote (overman), yet he was forced to resign himself to the level of vicarious experience only, a poor substitute for the real. Ill health required that he resign his professorship and in 1879 he set about to travel, broaden his experiences and seek if possible a cure for his dyspeptic condition. The "leave of absence" was to last a decade. In Turin, Italy, he began to lose his mind, collapsed and was returned to Basle and placed in a psychiatric clinic. He was suffering the ravages of syphillis. From Basle he went to his mother's home for care. When she died, he was cared for by his sister Elizabeth at Weimar. Suffering delusions of grandeur, he wrote the King of Italy, the Pope and others and signed himself, "The Crucified." He died at his sister's home. It is ironic that while his fame became known in his own lifetime, he could not have a clear conception of that fact.

Nietzsche's writings are many but are difficult to decipher, for frequently they are incomplete and aphoristic. Among his works are *Birth of Tragedy* (an analysis of Greek paideia and its sense of tragedy combined with its affirmation of life. His *Human, All—Too—Human* constitutes a reflection of the limitation of the human condition, coupled with early thoughts on morality. Beyond *Good and Evil* presents a fuller treatment of the two major types of morality, that of the masses vs. that of the aristocrat. *Joyful Wisdom* ushers in the announcement of the death of God and his *So Spoke Zarathustra* carries on this theme and develops the full notion of the *overman* (*Übermensch*) sometimes mistranslated as as Superman. His *Will to Power* provides an apology for power and describes its characteristics. Various other pieces are only loosely tied together, if at all.

Critique of the Times

Let's begin this section by taking a long hard look at our own age. We will do so from a Nietzschean perspective in order to get a "feel" for his thought.

Is our age an age of excellence or one of mediocrity? To find the answer, we must look at rock music, pop art, dress requirements, a lowering of academic standards, a loss of shame, blood and horror movies geared to the largest audiences of teenagers and at the mindless commercials of TV. Think about the last time you heard a worthwhile homily (sermon), enjoyed Church services with an organ and a choir instead of with a guitar ensemble. Today everyone is an athlete, jogger, iron pumper, etc., a song composer, and a singer. The distinction between amateur and professional has been blurred. Graffiti is "in" and adorns wash rooms, subways and public buildings. TV programs are geared to the least common denominator and advertising features the anti hero— the blue collar worker who never achieves anything except "getting through" life. World population is a vital and honest concern but dole and welfare cases abound and increase. Over fifty percent of the births in many of our cities are illegitimate. The English language had been reduced to slang, mispronunciation and computerese. Everywhere decisions are made by committees which often are nothing more than examples of collective ignorance. There is no drawing room music and there no longer are drawing rooms.

We insist our leaders be "like us," and worry if they rise above the mob through polite mannerisms, insights and intelligence. We are tried by a jury of largely uneducated peers, rather than by experts. Our overall resources are limited but we refuse to raise questions about where best these might be applied. Should we spend them on the poor, the handicapped and in general on those who cannot or will not make a contribution to society? Even the word, "handicapped" has been replaced by "exceptional," so as not to offend, despite its being a fact of life. Special training funds for the gifted are not as available as those for the less than mediocre.

Where are the Rembrandt artists of today and the Da Vincis? Who is composing the beautiful Strauss waltzes and the powerful Messiah of Handel? Where are Professors who are Professors, i.e., those creative in their own ideas, and not merely communicators of someone else's ideas. Has not our age been one in which nearly everyone and everything has been leveled, as though reality is one gigantic union movement? Elitism and excellent have become "embarrassing" and "dirty" words. The vote of a brilliant mind has the same worth as that of an illiterate who also goes to the voting booth. Now, all of these charges involve some hyperbole, of course, but they are grounded. Is it democracy that grounds them, or is it only general decadence, symptomatic of a world crisis of culture?

In certain situations, we are willing enough to act strongly and do what must be done. In disaster nursing, for example, *triage* prevails. That is the practice of medics dividing casualities into three divisions. The first is those "who can make it on their own," the second that of those "who need help, but if provided will survive," and thirdly, those who "won't make it" even though they get help. Given the limited resources of that situation, it is clear what action must be taken and who must be tended. The lower third are expendable, and the first group can fend for themselves.

In his own time, Nietzsche saw these same kinds of issues, albeit with some variation. He termed this condition of culture and the world—*nihilism*. It is the malaise of reality and Nietzsche preached that all was in vain, nothing had meaning. For example, we continue a nuclear arms race, knowing all the while that it is not the answer to peace, but to world destruction. Knowing this truth, we still remain hypocritical and hold on to the false. (In many respects, Nietzsche anticipates Albert Camus's *The Stranger* and Sartre's *Nausea*.) Nihilism then is "a contemplation of the 'in vain,' not only the belief that everything is worthy of going to destruction; one applies one's hand and send it there." This is not Schopenhauer's pessimism, however. It is Nietzsche's realism and it generates optimism in a strange kind of salvation. With nothing but chaos to begin with, we have been given the opportunity to impose and create values—our own values.

Addressing the Issue

For Nietzsche, it is Christianity which is largely responsible for what might be termed our crisis of culture. Christianity promotes mediocrity for it favors the weak, the old, the sick. It negates life by being mournful toward the world, by encouraging our separation from things of the world. It insists on dogmatism and this stifles creativity.

To correct this we must imitate nature, for nature favors life and the strong. It shakes out the weak and never invents the "State" which is the protector of the "superfluous ones." Nature exhibits little else than the will to survive, under any and all conditions. It will modify itself, as plants and animals characteristics change from desert habitats to those of the tundra, but always it seeks to survive. It some ways, the recent study called sociobiology seems to confirm this.

Also as a partial remedy for our decadence, we can model the early Greeks, before the time of Socrates and Plato. There we see the kind of culture which produces the superior man whom Nietzsche admired as the hope of humanity. It was a culture of the agon, the contest in which the superior won out. It was a culture that was balanced and two sided rather than one sided like our own. There we paid homage to both Apollo, the god of reason, and Dionysus (Bacchus) the god of passion. (Both are displayed in the book and movie, *Zorba the Greek*.) Despite man's fates imposed by the gods, man affirmed life and struggle. They had the courage to be and to be their own masters.

What Must Be Done?

For Nietzsche the gods no longer deserve a place in the world of man. We have entered the *Götterdamerung*—the twilight of the gods. Man will be the new god and he will become so through his will to power. Ours is a time then when intellect has had its day and discovered its own impoverishment and its own impotence. Will must now take over. Out of this matrix will rise the overman (*Übermensch*), a kind of mythic ideal toward which those who have the courage can strive. Aspects of the overman have shown themselves at various times in various cultures. All are self justifying through their very strength. Whether we speak of the American mountain men of the West in the early 19th century, or the *laissez-faire* lords of capitalism in the latter half of the same century, each is the same. They owe duty only to their equals. They recognize their equals as "good," i.e., worthy, enemies. Cf. Holmes and Moriarity in the stories of Conan Doyle. The new man is the architect in Ayn Rand's *The Fountainhead*, who flouts what the masses and mediocrity demand and blows up his creation rather than let them desecrate it.

We have been given the direction in which to proceed from the prophetic pronouncements of Zarathustra, (the Persian god, Zoraster) who running down the mountain toward man declares, "*Gott ist tot!*"—*God is dead.*

For Nietzsche, then, and contrary to Marx, it is not the masses that make the difference in history, it is the individual, the strong individual. The quest of that individual always is power and this in turn creates value as well as meaning. He may never fully succeed in his quest for absoluteness, for as Nietzsche observes, we are "human, all-too-human." Yet he knows that "what does not kill him will make him stronger."

The overman sees society as a series of plateaus or levels, each group looking down with disdain on the group below itself. Men are not equal, vs. Christianity's teachings. Some are strong and some are weak and it is the place of the former to assume rightful superiority. Even Aristotle thought some are born to be slaves for this is nature at work in its will to survive. The elite or overman is like an unbroken mustang who roams wild and free, overseer of all he surveys.

Mass Morality and Aristocratic Morality

Nietzsche draws an ironic picture of a person finding a herd of sheep and a lone shepherd. The newcomer asks, "Who's in charge here? . . . " Reflecting on this we must accept, says Nietzsche, that there is a double morality that obtains in the world, that of the herd (*Herden*—masses) and that of the aristocrat (the *Herrn*—elite). What is a vice to one is a virtue to the other. For example: humility in the masses is seen by the strong as hypocrisy, while pride and arrogance in the elite is seen by the weak as sinful. Machiavelli's *The Prince* is a true aristocrat for he exercises a true will to power. He knows what he is about and is decisive in doing it. In some ways, Dostoevsky's story of the Grand Inquisitor also portrays this distinction of the masses and the *cognoscenti*—those in the know. There the Grand Inquisitor tells Christ that the masses cannot bear the truth. He says, "I have corrected thy work and have founded it on miracle, mystery and authority. And men again rejoiced that they were led like sheep."

The herd sees the world in terms of true and false measured in some kind of objective terms; the elite understands that what is true is true only because it promotes life. What is false is false because it denigrates life. The herd wants to be free of its freedom (cf. Sartre's bad faith and his inauthentic man). Like sheep, they want to be led. The elite prides his freedom, for like fire stolen from the gods, with it he can now become his own god. In so doing he will create a trans-valuation of values. Western values are already dead or dying and the elite, but not the herd realize this. This is why in Marcel's terms, (as is indicated later) "there is an inverse proportion between optimism with respect to technology and a rise of philosophies of despair."

Elite morality understands the killing of unfit infants in Sparta and the abandoning of the old by Indians and Eskimos. Resources must be seized by the best and be used *for the best*. In more contemporary terms, one might ask if governmental research money is best given only to elite universities with top scientists or to mediocre ones who will never produce a Nobel prize winner.

Yet despite the appearances, Nietzsche's call is not to deprecate the downtrodden so much as it is to have each of us realize to the fullest our own potentialities. The examples he employs are used simply to illustrate his point.

Lastly, the elite will recognize that man's eternity is in time, whose endless repetition witnesses and constitutes an *eternal return*. There is a fatalism in Nietzsche's vision of the world, but it can be overcome through willing that fatalism. In many ways it parallels the confrontation Nietzsche faced in his own physical pain and mental anguish.

All in all, Nietzsche serves as a provocateur and seeks not disciples or imitators. What Soren Kierkegaard was to the sacred and Christian order, Nietzsche was to the order of the profane. In some way, Kierkegaard's praise of the apostle was Nietzsche's praise of the genius.

It is noteworthy that Nietzsche's thought mirrors several important ideas of Freud. Both accepted the vision that man's discontent was in large measure due to the bridle put upon him by civilization. Both accepted a basic savagery beneath the surface of man's appearance. It is fair to say that Nietzsche was a man of excess, but not in his life, which was moderate, only in his thoughts. He was little interested in presenting a system of philosophy and this plus his emphasis on will has caused many to place him in the camp of existentialism.

A Word of Caution

For decades after his death, Nietzsche was looked upon by the world at large as espousing what was to become a justification for the Hitler era. He was reviled as anti-Semitic and accused of extolling German nationalism. In fact, Hitler himself so interpreted Nietzsche. Yet nothing could be further from the truth. What brought this misconception about was one of the strange detective mysteries in the history of philosophy. The story follows.

As we indicated, Nietzsche was given to the care of his mother when he became mentally incompetent. Accordingly, all of his writings were in her legal charge. Upon her death, they reverted to Elizabeth, his sister, who was now their sole possessor. Elizabeth was enamoured with a Herr Forster, whom she later married. He was a high school teacher who was caught up in the movement against the Jews. He persuaded her (whether with ease or difficulty, we know not) to release only those works and excerpts from the Archives which appeared favorable to the cause of anti-Semitism and German nationalism. Even forgery was used in changing the names of persons to whom some of Neitzsche's letters were addressed. Quotations were taken out of context, and some were actually invented to further the Nazi cause.

This travesty of justice was uncovered through the laborious work of Dr. Karl Schlecht who edited a revised edition of Nietzsche's *Werke*. He restored Nietzsche to his rightful place as a humanistic philosopher of culture. Far from being anti-Semitic, Nietzsche praised the intellectual gifts of the Jews and readily and rigorously condemned the German nationalism, which he regarded as symptomatic of the nihilism he confronted.

It pays us to read Nietzsche carefully then and in his entirety, so that we can come to appreciate what his thoughts really were, instead of how for so many years they came to be misinterpreted. That such was the case is ironic for as Nietzsche himself wrote, "There are no facts, there only are interpretations."

FRIEDRICH NIETZSCHE

Review Questions

1. Explain and discuss the culture of Europe in the 19th century.
2. Discuss: Do you think our personal background has an influence on the way we think? and the thoughts we think?
3. What does Nietzsche mean by Nihilism? What is your position toward such an outlook?
4. Name three different works of Nietzsche and indicate the theme of each.
5. What are your views on Herd and Elite morality? Do people who lead, practice what they preach? Do they share your basic morality?
6. What does Nietzsche mean by designating our time as the twilight of the gods? Can you document this in some way?
7. Is is possible that Nietzsche failed to see in his criticism of Christianity, that weakness may well be its strength? Discuss.
8. What are some weak points of democracy in developing leaders? What are some strong points? Is there a difference between theory and practice as to which government best promotes the good of society? Discuss.
9. Give examples of the Dionysian man and the Apollonian man? Which is closer to your own life style?
10. Discuss the meaning of the phrase, "God is dead." Have you ever felt this to be true on occasion?

Special Thought Question

Ours is a rich society, yet nonetheless its resources are limited and finite. Is there any difference between a just, an equitable and a best distribution of resources? What are the merits and demerits of each?

BIBLIOGRAPHY

Primary Source: The Philosophy of Nietzsche. (New York: The Modern Library, c. 1954). (Contains helpful introduction and five of Nietzsche's best known works.)

Secondary Source: Nietzsche: Philosopher of Culture. Frederick Copleston (New York: Barnes and Noble, 1975). An objective appraisal by a distinguished historian of philosophy.

13
WILLIAM JAMES (1842–1910)

"Materialism only offers a sea of disappointment; religion offers a world of promise." The Varieties of Religious Experience

American Pragmatism

If we could single out a thinker who typifies the American mentality and attitude and who, indeed, has helped to shape that attitude, the choice of many would be William James. He certainly is the first American whom Europeans recognized as a genuine philosopher. It is no exaggeration to say that he conveyed the spirit of America abroad. Indeed, he lectured in Britain and received much of his fame from those lectures which later came to be published as *The Varieties of Religious Experience*.

The philosophy which he elaborated and which is almost identified with his name came to be known as pragmatism. It was not so much a system, for James had a revulsion for systems in philosophy. He thought they were too closed-in and resistant to the new which everyday enters into our lives. Rather, pragmatism was a variety of insights into the human condition of psychological moral and religious experiences. Each of us has a philosophy within ourselves and it was this James sought to nurture. As he wrote, "The philosophy which is so important in each of us is not a technical matter, it is our more or less dumb sense of what life honestly and deeply means. It is only partially got from books."

To a large extent, his own philosophy of pragmatism is a reaction against previous European and Greek philosophy that was always highly speculative in nature. Their concerns always seemed to be of things that had no immediate and no practical consequences for making life more fruitful and enjoyable. They worried over whether we could obtain Absolute Truth, whether we knew reality or only our own idea of it, whether one could prove or disprove the existence of a God, etc. Eventually, going through the grist mill of various philosophers through the ages, an

120

impasse was reached on practically every one of these issues. Philosophy was "dead in the water" or to use a land based metaphor, could not progress because of this roadblock. Quite literally, James asked what difference it made whether they were right or wrong—life move on anyways. The thing to do was to get off of "dead center" and take a different look at what one understands by truth, value and such other abstract concepts.

Besides America was a different world and had different needs. It was a hustling and bustling country. Roads had to be made, bridges had to be constructed. Industries had to get started and cities had to get built. As Americans, we had no time for useless speculation. Our forte was action and praxis and our philosophy should reflect that. James' philosophy mirrored this.

With his background in medicine and psychology, he argued (almost too simply, thought some) that truth is what works. This became the main thesis of pragmatism. If an idea is operationally effective, that is, produces wholesome and fruitful results, that is all that we mean by truth. This is all it means and is more than enough for life. What is false, then, is false because it does not produce good results, it does not make one happy. To put it coldly, and boldly, James sought the experiential or "cash" value of ideas. (What could be more American?) Yet by this phrase he meant their practical worth, for he condemned vigorously those who sought only the "bitch goddess of success." His meaning of truth, i.e., that which is useful and valuable must never be interpreted narrowly, for it was as broad as life itself.

Biographical Data

Oddly enough, James did not start off his career as a professional philosopher. Originally, his main contributions were in the area of psychology. Even later, his psychological theories provided the essential basis for his philosophy of pragmatism. But in order to understand James' psychological and philosophical positions, it is helpful to know something about his life and background, for their influences partly condition his views.

James was born in New York City in 1842. His brother, Henry James, some thirty years his senior, was to achieve fame as a literary figure. Among Henry's novels are *The Golden Bowl* and *The Turning of the Screw.* It is often said that Henry wrote like a philosopher, while William wrote like a novelist. Be that as it may, both of the James' were gifted writers.

Well to do, the James family traveled extensively and William came to feel equally at home in Europe as in America. In fact, Henry renounced his American citizenship to become an English national.

Besides studying in Europe, where William became gravely ill for awhile, William also studied at Princeton and Harvard, eventually receiving degrees from both institutions. At Harvard he met many famous men including Teddy Roosevelt, Oliver Wendell Holmes, George Santayana and Josiah Royce. With some he became intimate friends. An M.D., William taught psychology for a time at Harvard. There he became closely associated with Charles Sanders Peirce, through their mutual membership in the Harvard Metaphysical Club. Peirce, a physicist and later a great influence on the movement of "linguistic analysis," was interested in *meaning;* James was interested in *truth.* Some friction arose between them and Peirce became unhappy with James' use of the term, "pragmatism," which Peirce had coined. Accordingly, Peirce now called his own position, "pragmaticism," "a name," he said, "which is so ugly, no one will steal it."

William James gave a number of Gifford lectures at the University of Edinburgh in Scotland around the turn of the century. With these, we see his transition from psychologist to philosopher. His fame in the latter area was even to exceed his reputation as a psychologist. Many of his ideas were further developed and applied to educational theory and practice by the well-known American educationalist, John Dewey. Dewey's interest was in *value* and he saw James' ideas as instruments for practical action.

Investigation into Religious Experiences

James had always exhibited an interest in religious experience, probably due in part to his father who was fascinated by the notions of Emmanuel Swedenborg, a Scandinavian spiritualist. Some Swedenborgians claimed the new religion could offer communication between this world and the next. James was keenly aware of the psychological effect religious experience could have on the believer or non-believer. He explored these in great detail describing them in typical prose as "healthy minded" or as "sick minded" religion. His theories attempted to explain, and in many cases, to justify religious experience at the psychological level. The reader of James is impressed with his thoroughgoing studies in *The Varieties of Religious Experience* and his well written *The Will to Believe.*

Let's take an example of what James means here. To a person possessing confidence or faith, accomplishing a particular task may be relatively easy. The confidence will help him achieve his goal. But if a person faces a task which he doubts he is able to achieve, he stands a pretty good chance of failure. Faith or confidence can work wonders for a person and this is what religion gives to many. Hence, since religion has useful consequences, that is, has fruitful effects, it can be termed pragmatically true. In short, faith can produce facts. Hospitals frequently witness this when some of their patients who vitally need a blood transfusion refuse to grant such permission on the grounds of religious conviction opposing this. In many cases, to the astonishment of the doctors, the patients recover. The phrase "Faith works wonders," is not an empty one; rather it encourages the fullness of life.

What enables one to have faith is not so much the intellect of man as it is the will. In the rationalism of European philosophy from Descartes on, most philosophers ignored the important role of will, but with Kierkegaard, Nietzsche and James it takes on new significance. (One recalls Chesterton's remarks apropos this: "When a child is born, there is not so much the presence of a new intellect in the world, so much as there is the eruption of a new will." All parents know this fact of life!)

It is will, then says James that allows us choice; it is the will that can *will to believe.* Indeed, it *must* will to believe. After all, there are enough fence sitters who because they can't get absolute evidence for deciding this or that, never make a decision. They posture under the aegis of agnosticism whose prayer is, "Oh God, if there is a God, save my soul, if I have a soul!"

But in most instances in personal life, we can't wait for final answers, should there even be any. What one must do is to cut the Gordian knot of indecision and choose. Recall Kierkegaard on this point! What if my choice is wrong, one might say—a question that proceeds from the mind set of the agnostic? James replies that to a large extent, the vigor with which the choice is made, should *make* that the right choice. In following up upon that choice, one will *make* it the best. Let us say one has a choice of careers between being a doctor of medicine or a lawyer. Either would be acceptable. The thing to do is to choose one vigorously and one can bet, says James, that in later years, when the fruits of that choice manifest themselves, one will be convinced it was the right one. Truth is always judged by what is subsequent, by what flows from one's choice. Thus the back of speculative agnosticism was broken through appeal to will rather than intellect. In asserting itself, will leaves agnosticism to worry itself to death.

We can see in this kind of advice that James moves away sharply from Old World traditions and into an American framework of thought. Carrying the "weight of the past" can be deadening to a future oriented people. We must change from being spectators to participants, from viewing the world as substance to seeing it as process, from forgetting about yesterday to anticipate instead a tomorrow. From this it follows that the source of belief in religion is not important; where it leads is the real concern. Fruits, not roots should be the criteria of truth.

What Religion Can Do

Now, according to James, religion should vary with the individuals who possess it. If we are sick souls (and James, when ill in Paris, put himself in this category; he was subject to fits of depression and more than once the thought of suicide seriously crossed his mind), we need a religion of salvation which consoles us. If we are weak-willed, we need a religion of inspiration; if we are among the downtrodden, we need a religion which offers rewards in a future life, since it's apparent we can't have them here. In James' view, religion makes easy and happy, that which for practical purposes, is necessary anyway. As opposed to materialism which only offers "a sea of disappointment," religion offers "a world of promise."

Following upon this is the need to revise our notions of religion and the kind of God it offers as we go through the stages of life. The child, the youth, the adult and the oldster all need different religions and different Gods. What served well at one point of life may be inconsequential now at a new stage. Throughout his writings on religion (and a most interesting section is his views on the psychology of conversion—we do not convert *to the good* so much as *away from the evil*), James is fascinated by the "power of prayer." Speculatively, it does not make sense. Practically, it consoles, it gives hope, it can be an expression of joy and all in all, since it works wonders, it therefore is true. Of course we must remember the identification of truth with value for James. As a practical matter, James would agree that it is best to take up Pascal's "wager" about God. If we believe, we have everything to gain, even if such a God does not exist. If we do not believe, and there is a God, we have everything to lose. Why not be on the safe side?

Quite obviously, James was concerned almost exclusively with the psychological effects of religious feeling, rather than with the genuine reality of the object of religion. He reminds us very much of the "positive-thinking-approach" of some preachers today, who appear to be concerned almost entirely with the psychological lift their sermons give to others (or possibly to themselves). While much of this is sound psychology, the question can be raised if it is legitimate to reduce religion to psychology. It is not a difficult mistake to make—confusing statements about the *ideas* of *God* and statements about the *reality behind* the ideas of God. James seems prone to move in the former direction. Yet if we accept James' principles we must go along with him. One of those principles is that there is no hidden "reality" beyond the face value of things.

Nonetheless, he scoffs at the "medical determinists" who explain St. Paul's vision by "a discharging lesion of the occipital cortex." The same scorn is given those who see St. Theresa as "an hysteric," Francis of Assisi as "an hereditary degenerate," or George Fox's discontent with his age as accounted for by "a disordered colon." It is true, says James, that many religious are neurotics, but this does not itself answer the question whether or not what they claim to experience is true.

All in all, James is telling us that reality is our perception; if we are unhappy with it, we should change our perception. This is effected primarily by will. The problem of will and freedom, as we know, was wrestled with for some time before James saw that paradoxically the will was free because it could will (i.e., believe) it as free. Furthermore, such experiences as *regret* reinforce the evidence of freedom. In all of this problem of freedom he thanks the influence of Charles Renouvier.

But James also warns us that religion may produce certain harmful effects. This is especially true if we become guilty of *over-beliefs*. One such overbelief in which he himself admits to entertaining, is belief in One God Who is Absolute; another is the belief in only one religion as true.

Still another effect of some religions which might be viewed as harmful according to James' principles, would be the forcing of one person's religious views on another who does not wish it or who has no need of it. For example, a great deal of internecine warfare was carried on between Catholics and Protestants as to how one must interpret the mystery of the Mass at the time of Consecration. Was it to be explained by transubstantiation (the Catholic position) or by transsignification (the Protestant view)? James would ask what difference it made, for neither Protestant nor Catholic communicant even knew what the dispute was about yet both received a fuller life by the ritual. (It may be questionable whether even the theologians knew what they were about! Yet terrible persecution followed by those holding to transsignification rather than the other.)

A Radical Empiricism

James' philosophical views went contrary to idealism, particularly against the Hegelian Idealism of the American, Josiah Royce. James called his own position a *radical empiricism* and *pragmatism*. As he saw it, traditional empiricism had plenty of facts but no religion. On the other hand, traditional rationalism had plenty of religion, but no facts. His own system of pragmatism would combine the merits of both, yet omit their respective defects. Pragmatism could be used to settle philosophical disputes by seeing which side had more fruitful consequences, and therefore, greater truth.

Since reality is always changing, we can never achieve absolute truth. Indeed there is no need to do so! Rather, James advises, it is better to accept things at their "face value." In fact, we have no other workable alternative. (One is reminded of the woman who approached the British philosopher and mathematician, Lord Bertrand Russell, "Lord Russell," she exclaimed, "I finally accept reality!" His cryptic reply to her was, "Madame, you had better!")

James then regards himself as a realist, rather than an idealist, for it is more profitable, that is, it is more convenient and fruitful to accept that we *know* reality, than to deny it. But reality is not a bloc universe and we must always be ready to change our stance with respect to it.

Values

In light of the unattainability of absolute truth the best that we can achieve are value judgements. If nature is changing, then asks James, "What has concluded that we might conclude in regard to it?" We must be satisfied with what appears to work best, yet at the same moment, be ready and open to new truths, or new avenues of action which might be even more fruitful.

Values in such a system are obviously not ready made or absolute. Quite the contrary, they are always changing. To a large extent, it is *we* who *make* such values. Often it is *we ourselves who make things work*, and hence, *make them true* for us. Truth is not so much to be discovered, then, for it is always in the making. The same might be applied to goodness and beauty as well. Truth is clearly not a property of things or ideas; rather, it is something which happens to things or ideas. It is something which must always be verified, directly or indirectly by someone. Obviously then, in this system, all truth must be related to a knower. We do not so much love a thing because it is valuable, but it is valuable because we love it.

Faith Promotes Truth

Faith is often the only thing which makes a result *become* true. Take the example of a person who is about to attempt jumping over a crevasse. If he is convinced he will make it, that faith will give him the extra push needed to get to the other side; yet if he is convinced that he can't jump over, he is liable to falter and make an unsuccessful leap right into the abyss. Faith helps us to make decisions so necessary for successful living. After all, seldom is the evidence fully compelling for this or that action. What we must do in such cases is decide, will to believe, and act.

Psychologically, of course, faith is always *faith in someone else's faith* according to James. That is why it is so important to reveal to another our confidence in him. Thus, in not letting us down, he will not be letting himself down. What we witness here then is one more instance of faith producing fact.

In a way we can find ourselves quite sympathetic to James' position. The reason that any Christian believes in the Father is because their faith is rooted in the faith of Christ who believed in the Father.

Continuing these views, James points out that we really believe what we *want to believe*. Conversely, we often refuse to believe what we do not wish to believe. It is much as a mother might refuse to believe her soldier son has been killed in action, for she does not want to accept it. As James puts it, "We can be convinced by logic only if we are first disposed to its conclusions." In this we hearken back to the Pascalian tradition of the "logic of the heart." And who can deny that "Heart has its reasons that reason cannot understand?" As James puts it, "If your heart won't let you, your mind can't make you!

Some Reverse Thinking and Acting

Keen observer of human character, James points out that contrary to popular opinion, *what we are*, largely determines *what we think*. In other words, we seldom become what we think we should be, rather, we tend to possess the views we have, because we are already that kind of person. In this respect, James delineates two types of personality, the tough-minded and the tender-minded. The empiricist represents the former, the idealist the latter. I believe there was a bit of both in James. Although he was no friend of Teddy Roosevelt, both did agree on the need for being vigorous, physically and mentally. Both opposed a "world of clerks." It was a struggle that promoted life and this theme is pursued in James' famous *The Moral Equivalent of War*.

Another view of William James which goes counter to popular opinion is the theory of emotions which has come to be regarded in psychology as the James-Lange theory of emotion. Basically that view is this. Many have believed that we first perceive an object (such as a bear), then produce an emotion (become afraid) and finally react to this experience (run). James would view it as in the following order. First the object presents itself (the bear), then we react (run) and only now do we produce the emotion (become afraid). To oversimplify it, we do not run so much because we are afraid, rather, we are afraid because we run. Qualifiedly, the view has certain obvious merits, for if we allow ourselves to "go to pieces," our fear can be lessened considerably. (However, in the case of seeing a ferocious bear, I'm *afraid* that in most cases our emotions would *run away with us!*)

One final word about William James, the great American psychologist-philosopher who died in 1910. He claimed that "A difference, to be a difference, must make a difference!" On such grounds, we could agree that James' philosophy of pragmatism was different, for his ideas have made considerable differences in the history of thought and action.

WILLIAM JAMES

Review Questions

1. Approximately when did James live?
2. What was the first discipline in which he was trained and received his fame?
3. How did this first discipline come to bear on his philosophy?
4. James, Peirce and Dewey are three famous American thinkers. James was interested in ideas from the viewpoint of *truth*, whereas the interest in ideas for Peirce and Dewey were in _____ and _____, respectively.
5. Discuss: Can different religions all be true for James?
6. What does James mean when he claims that faith is faith in someone else's faith?
7. What are some dangers of "overbeliefs?"
8. Are values stable or changing for James? Why?
9. Explain: Things are not true, but they become true; truth is always in the making.
10. Give an example of what James meant in saying: To be a difference, it must make a difference.

Special Thought Question

What would you characterize as a "sick minded" religion and a "healthy-minded" religion? Why?

BIBLIOGRAPHY

Primary Source: *Pragmatism and Other Essays.* (New York: Washington Square Press, 1963). (Most of the major ideas of James are to be found in this collection.)

Secondary Source: *William James.* Edward Carter Moore (New York: Washington Square Press, 1966). (An easy reading overview on James' ideas concerning religion, psychology and philosophy.)

14
JEAN–PAUL SARTRE (1905–1976)

"Value is nothing else than the meaning you choose."
Existentialism

Atheistic Existentialism

Jean-Paul Sartre is probably one of the most complex yet popular philosophers of all time. The titular head of the movement, existentialism, his fame outlived its fame, for existentialism now is history, whereas the ideas of Sartre are still vital. Incredibly versatile with his pen (he titled an autobiography of his youth, *The Words*), he wrote plays, such as *No Exit*, penetrating psychological studies as *The Emotions*, works of social criticism as *The Anti-Semite and the Jew*, edited an intellectualist newspaper, *Les Temps Moderne* and authored the profound book on ontology, *Being and Nothingness*. He was also the first person in history to refuse the Nobel Prize in literature, when offered to him in 1965. To accept it, he said, would be to permit himself to be "institutionalized" as a writer. Accepting such a bourgeois status, would betray his anti-institutional values. Who is this man and what are some of his important ideas?

Biographical Notes

Sartre was born in Paris in 1905. A number of relatives, such as Albert Schweitzer, the famed organist turned medical missionary in Africa, already were distinguished. A professional philosopher, Sartre showed especial interest in Husserl and Heidegger whose works he studied at the French Institute in Berlin. Their development of the phenomenological method was to exercise a lasting influence on Sartre. (This method involves an attempt to lay bare and describe the structure of consciousness and the world as constituted in part by this structure.) Sartre's descriptions here of shame, anxiety, etc, are considered classic.

He earned the doctorate, taught at Le Havre, then took a professorship at Lyces Condorcet in Paris. The year was 1935. It was the time of a worldwide economic depression and the beginnings of the Hitler era. Sartre's novel, *Nausea* (1957) reflected this catastrophic period. In it, all reality seemed so absurd, so disillusioning. It was Sartre's own vision for shortly thereafter, he found himself fighting in the war, without knowing quite why.

Taken prisoner early in the conflict, Sartre was released in 1941 and joined the Resistance movement, writing for that organization. In 1943, he wrote a play entitled *The Flies*. It was a play encouraging French patriotism, yet urging patience to await the coming liberation. It passed the unwary eye of a German censor board and caused considerable embarrassment to the Germans when it played in public. With it, Sartre's popularity waxed. His classic work *Being and Nothingness* also appeared about this time. The absurdity of things continued to impress him and he took to heart the story of the French Algerian, Albert Camus, who told of a war hero captured by the enemy and condemned to a public hanging. At least, thought the hero, he could die in witness to his belief in his ideals and perhaps be emulated by others. As it happened, he died of the flu in his jail cell. (One is reminded of the vast numbers of unknown "draft resisters" of the Viet Nam era, who, caught up in a *cause celébre*, thought they would bring attention to the "righteousness" of their cause; they only languished in jail, abandoned by all except their families.)

After the war, Sartre frequented old haunts in the student sector of Paris, the Latin Quarter. There at the *Cafe Deux Magots*, he found a ready audience for his ideas which appeared to the world as pessimistic and nihilistic, but to his young followers only as realistic. Whatever the case, his philosophy caught and nourished the mood of returning soldiers, a generation of antiheroes. It was a mood, which although formless, expressed a restlessness and dissatisfaction with the established order of a bourgeois society that now that the war was over expected to go back to "business as usual." But Sartre and others saw those values as sterile, as did many of our own Viet Nam vets. The society and religions which promoted those, even science was suspect—had proven untrustworthy. Such a society had proven untrustworthy as the last five years had shown. They needed to be exposed and a non-institutional substitute (the individual) put in their place. Here then was the point of departure for a new philosophy—the individual and his irreducible freedom in a world of absurdity.

Man, Value and the World

For Sartre, there are two kinds of beings, *subjects* and *objects;* free beings (being for itself) and beings fully determined (being in itself). Both are hostile and threaten to engulf each other. When I am born, I am nothing, that is, no-thing. It is because I am no thing and that I am free that I can make myself what I will be. My freedom is like a *vent*, a hole in my being which lets me escape the world of objects or fully determined things. In a sense, my ego trails behind me, for when I act, each act becomes other than myself, now that it has become an event and something objectified. My nature then never is constituted but always is in the making.

As Karl Marx pointed out that man creates himself through his work, so I am the creator of myself through my choices and actions, i.e., my freedom. I am the sole creator of meaning and value. Value is nothing more "than the meaning you choose," says Sartre. For example, a teen-ager who buys a car buys it for joyriding; an adult purchases it for more functional reasons, such as transportation to and from work. My overall task in life, then, is to invent values and to live by these. This constitutes my *project*, my forward thrust into meaning and time.

Everywhere I experience the hostility of the world, thrown into it as it were, without rhyme and reason. It's like being "given the ball" and told that I now must run with it, when I never asked for it in the first place. How absurd to be told I am absolutely free and then to have no choice into coming into the world itself! The world then threatens me and tries to swallow me up as a drop of honey falling back into the jar from whence it came. Society's institutions try to mold me into their image instead of letting me be what I am, a free being. Only what it is, the object (being in itself) has no potentialities. It is rigid, massive, still and complete. "A rose is a rose is a rose . . . " But because I am free, I can develop; I can be a devil or an angel. Indeed, I can even—indeed I must—take the place of God!

Man and Society

Unfortunately, it is not only the world that threatens me and promotes anxiety. Other human beings also do this, wittingly or unwittingly, for any relationship between humans involves a risk-taking commitment. To open myself fully to the other, to reveal my deepest subjectivity to the other is to risk all. Should I be the victim of an unrequited love, I probably never will allow myself to be fully open again.

What I am principally is a subject, a for-myself. But others look upon me as an object, a for-them. An instance is the single girl seen as a sex object by men looking for pleasure. In our relationships, we tend to establish a pecking order by objectivizing the other. An example will clarify this. Let us imagine two people coming into a waiting room where there is but one vacant chair. To offer the chair to the other is to capitulate him, to reduce him to your will. He is now under bond to you.

Sartre sees each human as attempting to immobilize the other to the status of a thing. This is accomplished by knowledge of the other—by the glance or the gaze *(regard)* of another. This is why we feel uneasy in the presence of a superior, for he can immobilize us, whereas we can be relaxed in the presence of a being lesser than ourselves.

It is as though we come upon another looking through the keyhole of a door at the occupants inside the room. At that moment the looker has been immobilized—uncovered—reduced to the status of a being in itself. The looker has lost his subjectivity and now senses guilt, for he has been revealed and is unable to justify himself. His experience is one of shame and his nakedness has been exposed. It is similar to the feeling that we are but a tool for the other, that we are only used by him, to be discarded when no longer of value. It makes of love a conquest instead of a surrender. This precarious situation promotes dread and anxiety, for in losing my subjectivity to the other, I lose my very being and freedom. I now am a slave, an object. We can understand the famous line from *No Exit*, "Hell is other people!" And we can now grasp the meaning of Mark Twain's observation, "Every man is a moon. Each has a dark side which he shows only to himself." This is why, Sartre claims, we like to see, without being seen. He uses as an example here the restaurants and bistros that populate a main street of Paris, the *Champs Elysée*. Each has a canopy over the front and patrons sit in the shaded and darkened back looking at those who promenade down the street. The passersby are objects for the patrons who see without being seen, i.e., who are not subject to the risk of being made an object of themselves.

In a certain way, this is why in our time a sense of shame somehow has slipped through the cracks. We have been objectified for so long by so many institutions that we question whether we even have subjectivity any longer. Instead of being what I make of myself, I am what the world and its conformist rules have made of me. I have lost my identity.

Man and God

Although Sartre maintains a postulatory atheism, that is, he assumes without proving, that there is no God, he tells us that once he confronted God. It was as a young boy, but the experience never returned. Those who made up the short lived "death of God" movement, i.e., Hamilton, Altizer and Van Buren, claimed an experience of the absence of God. Sartre only held to an absence of the experience of God. God was a most hidden being, if he existed, a veritable *Deus absconditus*.

Should we care to speak of God, the situation which obtains between men, also obtains between man and God, only more so. While some have claimed that if God did not exist, nothing would be possible, Sartre says the opposite. If God exists, nothing is possible for me, for I cannot be free, in effect, not be a human being. The reason is clear to Sartre, for if God is, He created everything according to a preconceived blueprint to which each must conform. This objectivization of myself is desubjectifying and dehumanizing. If God is, His gaze (knowledge), powerful enough to shame Adam and Eve and cast them from the Garden of Eden, penetrating enough to turn Lot's wife into a pillar of salt, would also petrify me and deprive me of my freedom and therefore my being as a man.

This is an important but round-about handling of the question of God's predestination of man, put into a contemporary context. As we see, the classic problems of philosophy are always there, for none has been fully resolved.

Sartre then cannot allow an interfering and competing God in his system and still preserve man's freedom. Yet Sartre is aware that without God there is no basis for value. Someone must take his place and it may as well be me. In this sense, man's passion to be God, is the opposite of Christ's God seeking to be man. I am the "baseless base of value." As such, I am solely responsible for my actions. This responsibility is not to others, however, as it is to myself. There would be little dread if I were responsible only to others, as an employee to his boss. This kind of responsibility I can always manage to pass off to another. My responsibility is to myself and this is nontransferable. I must be willing to live with it, for that's what it is to be human. Being human, then, is being "condemned to be free," to live in dread, to accept myself as the lone arbiter of value. It is a small wonder that many seek to be free of their freedom, for the burden is great. And the institution is always there to subsume them with its promise: "I will take care of all your needs, if *only* you obey me without question."

Sartre of course was a leading intellectual, not only of France but of the entire Western world. Intellectuals are perforce social critics and upsetters of the established order. In short they are thinkers! In a world run by mediocre bureaucrats, intellectuals will always constitute a threat and an eminent danger. It is clear that Sartre's writings come out of his own experience.

Authentic vs. Inauthentic Existence

Because I am free, I can choose to negate myself. I can wear a mask and hide behind this persona, never revealing myself. This is the life of a cop-out. This is inauthenticity and subhuman existence. The mask I wear may be one of authority—an army officer pulling rank on an enlisted man, or the policeman browbeating the urban black. I may hide behind the institution, behind someone else's values or someone else's image. The waiter, who chooses never to reveal himself beyond being a waiter is a case in point. In his work, he never puts his subjectivity on the line.

Another example is the airlines attendant, who plays her role (designed by someone else) perfectly. The voices of such attendants somehow all seem the same, the responses to questions are nearly always identical and the mannerisms similar, regardless of the airline or flight. "May I store your briefcase, sir?" "Would you like a magazine or a pillow?" "Have a pleasant flight now." "Have a nice day and thank you for flying . . . Airlines."

Things are little different with the voice over the loudspeaker, "This is your Captain . . ." Everything seems programmed and will brook no interference with the person behind the mask. That would be bad business! Such scenarios are repeated everywhere, with M.D.'s, Professors, store clerks, etc. Seldom do these persons ever reveal themselves, they show only their role. Each is hiding his and her own identity as a subject, presenting to the world for whatever aggrandizement it may take, the image of an object instead of the reality of a free subject. Those who live inauthentically are all guilty of bad faith, for they are only what others wish them to be.

Authentic existence, however, entails a full realization and acceptance of our human condition. It recognizes and welcomes the responsibility for all meaning and values. It recognizes that things are what I commit myself to, that whatever seeks to limit my choice, places a limit on me. It involves a willingness to raise the crisis of our existence, of steadfastly facing the moment of truth wich reveals us to ourselves for what we are.

Man then has no pre-established human nature. He is the ensemble of his actions, alone, yet with others in a hostile world. He is, in a word, pure freedom, a useless passion, magnificent in his absurdity.

Conclusion

Sartre is often accused of being selective in his examples, of seeing the pathological as what is normal. Where others see order, he sees absurdity and chaos; where others see love and beneficience, he sees only ulterior motives. The criticism is true, but only in part. Sartre calls for a humanism, albeit an atheistic one. He has given examples, both as writer and activist.

He has flirted with Marxism (as a humanism) and claimed that only it was a true philosophy. Existentialism was an ideology. Although Marxism, with its emphasis on the collective, seemed to go against the grain of Sartrean individualism, Sartre excused this as a temporary aberration of the moment in the struggle for human progress. He backed Algeria's independence and was on the intellectual side of Cuba in its running battles with the United States. However, his disenchantment with Marxism showed quite strongly with the onslaught of the Hungarian Revolution.

What we can say of Sartre is that he has focussed on man once again and that is to call attention to what is fundamental in philosophy. Largely because of Sartre (and phenomenology) man is and will continue to be, the focal point in philosophy for many years to come.

JEAN–PAUL SARTRE

Review Questions

1. Name a play or book written by Sartre.
2. How does Sartre's philosophy emerge in part from his own life experiences?
3. Why does Sartre see the world as absurd?
4. What is man's role in a world of absurdity?
5. What is the difference between a subject and an object?
6. If I am a subject primarily, why does my fellow man tend to see me as an object?
7. Why does Sartre deny there is a God, rather than remain an agnostic and say he can't be sure if there is or isn't a God?
8. What is "bad faith?" Give an example.
9. Explain: The essence of man lies in his no-thingness. Through his freedom, he creates what he will be.
10. Marx and Sartre may both be regarded as extolling a humanism. What are some differences between them and how can they both claim humanism?

Special Thought Question

If freedom is at the root of man's being, from what does freedom itself come?

BIBLIOGRAPHY

Primary Source: *No Exit, and Three Other Plays.* Tr. Stuart Golbert (New York: Alfred Knopf, 1946). (The easiest ways of understanding Sartre's basic themes are through his plays.)

Secondary Source: *Sartre.* Hazel Barnes (Philadelphia & New York: J.B. Lippincott Co., 1973). (Excellent overview and critique of Sartre by one who has translated into English Sartre's *Being and Nothingness.*)

15
GABRIEL MARCEL (1889–1973)

"We show what we have; we reveal what we are."
Philosophy of Existentialism

Personalism

Contemporary existentialism has often been characterized as espousing a philosophy of despair. But labels never tell the whole picture for within the existentialist movement other thinkers stress optimism and hope. They highlight not only the individual, but the individual in his relationship with others—a relationship which is perfective, not destructive. August Brunner and Martin Buber are examples. Another is the French philosopher Gabriel Marcel. Marcel is well known both inside and outside of philosophical circles for he has written essays, plays, composed music and has served as music critic. He has lectured all over the world and his philosophy is especially appealing to many, for it emerges out of his life experiences rather than out of an academic classroom. It speaks in a language that the nonprofessional can understand, the language of the depths of "Everydayness," the language of the person.

Biographical Sketch

Gabriel Marcel was born in Paris in 1889, the only child of a diplomat father. Marcel's mother died when Gabriel was quite young. Since his father frequently was away from home, Gabriel was raised in the matriarchial environment of an aunt and maternal grandmother. He was gifted and consequently always was the object of attention of the doting women. This attention often served to isolate him from the real and sometimes harsh outside world.

Each paper he brought home from school was discussed and praised by his caretakers who could not hide their pride in their charge. For them,

Gabriel was an object of delight and he responded to their affections by "enjoying" poor health, which kept him in and around the home more than other children. It was only until much later in life that he realized this attention stressed his *doing*, what he achieved, rather than his *being*, who he was.

He took his doctorate from Paris' Sorbonne in 1910 and throughout his life taught at various universities in France and throughout the world. Recognition was given to his work by his election to the prestigious French Academy. In World War I, he served as a Red Cross courier and it was this experience which changed his way of thinking and altered his outlook on the world. Previously he tended toward philosophical idealism and toward rationalism. They mirrored in some ways the comfortable but insulated days of his childhood, a time of sterile but hygenic atmosphere attended by near moral scrupulosity.

But now, in delivering messages of the death of a son killed in the war to grieving families, he came to appreciate another side of reality. Here he saw that reality had not to do with abstract theories but with concrete persons interacting with one another. Increasingly, his literary output began stressing the reality of person. The very titles of some of his plays and books make this explicit: *Broken World, A Man of God, Searchings, Metaphysical Journals, The Mystery of Being, Man Against Mass Society, Presence and Immortality, The Existential Background of Human Dignity*, etc.

He died in 1973 and until the very last, served as an effective critic of all those factors in modern society which tended to demean and depersonalize man. Since his philosophy centers around these themes, let us now explore them in more detail.

Critique of our Age

There are two ways of relating to the world, according to Marcel. One is to be passive and see the world as a kind of *spectacle* which lies before us. It was like looking out the window at things, but never venturing outside. Such an attitude corresponds roughly to the idealistic philosopher's temperament. (Here, Marcel echoes John Dewey's critique of early Greek philosophy, namely, that we must interact with things and persons in order to know them, not just "stare" at them.)

The second way is to participate in reality and indeed to always stand at its very center. This latter is the proper place of man as person and all values in the world will then be relative to him. This should not surprise us for it is only with man that meaning has come into its fullest. Yet this applies not to man in isolation, but in communion with fellow man. As the Anglican clergyman poet, John Donne, expressed it, "No man is an island, each is a part of the main." Unfortunately, certain aspects of our present world, though not prohibiting such interpersonal relationships, do often mitigate against these and push us in opposite directions. Examples are the requirements for competition in all walks of life—sports, business, academe, etc. Another instance is the identification of a person with a number, whether it be one's Social Security number or a computer printout.

While technology itself is indifferent to human values, there often accompanies it a "spirit" of technology which unconsciously but insidiously tends to play down the worth of man. It promotes the view that man is only "a thing among things," a denizen of the lesser world. The expression, "caseworker" signifies this. The worker has to do with "cases" not persons.

Another example is technology's inherent thrust to develop only functional (computer type) relationships, rather than human ones. The results of this are detailed by another Frenchman, Jacques Ellul in *The Technological System*. As with myth and religion, Ellul sees the technological system as seeking totality and universality. This is bound to result in a depersonalization, for man "no longer lives in touch with the realities of the earth and the water, but with the realities of the instruments and objects forming the totality of his environment." No longer is thought (Hegel) the mediator between man and reality, it is now the technological system.

Genuine human relationships begin to go by the board, then. An example is a salesman taking a client to lunch. Obviously his interest lies not in human friendship but in aggrandizing the other to land a large order. The attitude of a large, powerful country in its dealings with a smaller one at its mercy is often the same. Because it can manipulate the small country, the large one feels that it thereby understands it.

Then, too, our society and humans within it, tends to be run on a timetable and budgetary basis. Nothing must be allowed to interrupt that orderly flow. We are gradually being turned into automatons and reversing the natural order by using the machine as the paradigm in relation to man. We compare the eye to the camera, the hand to a tool, the brain to the computer and think of a sunset like a beautiful painting. If any comparison is to be made (itself a risky venture), the terms of comparison should be reversed.

The "spirit" of technology is everywhere with its accompanying shadow of numerical "accountability." Even in college today the language is one of "input—output," and "cost effectiveness." The Administration's concern seems limited exclusively to "credit hours generated," "degree productivity," and "enrollment head counts." One would never think from these that a college has anything to do with students as persons!

Not even life and death escape this fascination for statistics and the quantitative. Life and death are important only as spectaculars, such as the airplane crash which kills 300 people. Yet the death of an old man in a lonely room is as important and authentic as that of those in the crash. Statistics seem to be all that matters. Ironically, one recalls the story about the statistician who drowned while crossing a river on the average only two feet deep!

In the interests of continuing efficiency, the technological spirit would finally produce the modular man, one who can always be replaced by another, as a kind of organic transplant. That such replacement is impossible in human relationships is patent as the following indicate: A young girl's prized doll from last Christmas is accidentally thrown away. The parents promise to get another "just like it." But there can be no such replacement because (as St. Exupery points out in *The Little Prince*) the doll lost is her doll. She has "tamed" it and has related herself to it.

The same might be said of a man whose wife dies. While he may remarry, the new wife can never serve as a *replacement* for the one who dies. An entirely new relationship will have to be set up between the two, for each person, as a person, is irreplaceable. In this sense, persons are not equal; they are different. Persons, for Marcel, are like God's designer collection. No two are alike. Each is unique.

Summing up the danger points he observed in our fragmenting world, Marcel put at the top of the list our desire to manipulate the whole earth and all living things within it. He castigated the increased belief that salvation rests simply upon the ploy of proper techniques, that friendship was essentially a matter of Dale Carnegie colonization of the other. He decried the tendency to replace the wise man and extol instead the healthy man well adapted to all situations. Our times, he wrote, have put symbols in place of reality, paper shuffling in place of work, speeches in place of therapy. We have been deluded into thinking that because we can classify something (for purposes of system control) we thereby understand it. In fact, says Marcel, such classification necessarily misses what is unique in each thing, for it touches only upon that thing's universal features. For example, to call this flower a rose is to say only what it has in common with all other roses. What one must remember is that "to classify the flower is not an exhaustive answer; in fact . . . it is no answer at all; it is even an evasion . . . it disregards the singularity of this particular flower. In asking what this flower is, it is as though my question had been interpreted as follows—'To what thing other than itself can this flower be reduced?' "

Those who have read St. Exupery's *Little Prince* will see the sting of Marcel's critique. There, a rose is not *a* rose, it is *my* rose, much as a child's dog is *his* dog. There is none like it in the world, for its meaning and value have been given to it alone, out of the child's love for it.

It is no wonder that we have at the same time, optimism with respect to technical progress and a rise in philosophies of despair.

The Corrective

Despite what might appear as a negative outlook, Marcel offers us the basis for seeing things in a positive light. All such grounds again center around greater insights and appreciation of the person. Person is unique for he lives on the threshold of two worlds, the material and the spiritual. He belongs to neither exclusively and thus may be termed an incarnate spirit.

What has happened to cause us this neglect of this most perfect of all creations, the person? Basically (and in the interest of simplification), we have equated things which need to be distinguished. Let us look at the following columns and reflect on the differences that obtain there:

Curiosity	Wonder
Wish	Hope
Science	Wisdom
Problem	Mystery
Acquaintance	Friend
Presents	Presence
Individual	Person
Having	Being

The list is too long to go over in detail and point to Marcel's explication of each, but let us take two items for a short elaboration. Both help reveal the thrust and style of Marcel's philosophy.

The first is the distinction between problem and mystery. For most, the terms seem interchangeable, yet to blur the distinction between the two is again to fall prey to an idealist and/or technological attitude. "A *mystery* is a problem which encroaches upon its own data, invading them, as it were, and thoroughly transcending itself as a simple problem." The *problem* is what is merely in front of me, a thing to be solved, a riddle or puzzle to be worked out. Once solved, I am through with it, such as finding the solution to the problem as to why my car won't start. Once solved (fixed), I can drive away and forget about it. The problem attitude never sees tragedies, only mistakes. As a problematic, evil is only something that stands in need of "correction:" it is a social or individual malfunctioning. Injustice can be righted by social techniques.

Mystery however, is not what is in front of me and apart from me, but something in which I am personally caught up. It demands involvement, my involvement. This is why people in love (a mystery) can fathom each other perfectly, whereas onlookers, cannot understand what they see in each other. We cannot have an appreciation of the mystery of evil or injustice as mystery (as minorities tell us), unless somehow we are "touched" by them and caught up in them. Drug addiction in a teenager may be viewed as a problem by a social worker, but to the parent of that youngster it is a mystery and sparks the agonizing question, "Why my son or my daughter?" Seen problematically, life is a mere burden of existence, a tedium of detail, a struggle to "get through the day." Grasped as mystery, however, it is a proclamation of victory over nothingness. In this sense, all life is truly amazing, no matter how malformed or deprived!

Let us now take the second example from our list cited above. It is that of the distinction between "Having" and "Being." It is absolutely fundamental for Marcel. To identify the two inevitably proves fatal for an appreciation of both persons and reality itself. We think of a person as really *"being* someone" only so long as he *"has* something." When he no longer has something, e.g., money, credit cards, influence, an important job, etc., he no longer is anyone. In the eyes of the world, he is a nobody.

The assumptions clearly show that we have placed all meaningfulness in the category of *having* something rather than in that of *being*. In such a world it is no wonder we neglect the poor, the sick, the aged, the imprisoned and the "non-functional." They share this in common—that they *have* nothing and so are viewed as of no worth. This is so universal a view that the world stood at attention and literally was shocked when a "nobody" won the Nobel Prize some years back. The "nobody" was Mother Teresa, the Yugoslav nun who works in India with the "nobodies" of the world. This simple nun, "a nobody," won the prize for all "nobodies!"

Yet an examination of the term "having" and "being" reveals more to us. We see there are different meanings of "having," gradations of "having" that begin to approach "being." For example, I can say I *have* a car, I *have* blond hair, I *have* a secret, I *have* a friend, I *have* a body. In each case, the "have" has come closer to "being" to the point that in the last, I may legitimately say, "I am my body." At the one end of the spectrum, "to have" meant "to possess," "to be able to dispose of," as in the case with a tool. At the other end, "to have," meant "to be."

This identification of myself with my body shows the strong empirical bent of Marcel's thought. Unless one can relate things to one's body, they must be regarded as suspect and quite possibly the product of an idealistic mentality. My body, then, is a subject and not just an object. The recent rash of "physical exercise" literature tends towards the view of my body as object, e.g., the phrase "me and my body," "take care of your body," etc. Such language suggests a return to the view of man as a soul within a container—a Platonic and Cartesian view. It ignores the flesh, blood and spirit that comprises a human being to make him a person, or in Marcel's terms, an "incarnated spirit."

Toward a Fuller Appreciation of Person

We are now prepared to see more into the meaningfulness that person brings to the world. And it is in his phenomenological reflections on the commonplace marks of the person that Marcel's thought is so revealing. To genuinely *have* a friend is to *be* a friend. A friend (unlike an acquaintance) does not so much bring his *presents* to the bedside of an ill person, as he brings his *presence*, his availability, his-self. Because we are persons, we can be friends, and it is the friend who invariably reveals me to myself. My friend is my alter-ego who brings out the latent best within me. As Marcel reminds us, "To have a friend is to have privileged access to a knowledge about myself." He is the one who awakens me to the wonderment (as opposed to curiosity) about myself in a way not otherwise possible, for the beloved evokes my willingness to sacrifice everything I have for my beloved—my life, if necessary. The mystery of friendship can be experienced when I ask, "How can this other person somehow be more at the center of my being that I am myself?" Here we see community, for "to be" is "to be with" the other.

Exploring this latter "withness" or presence, Marcel points out that it too has a variety of meanings. Two people standing at a bar are present to each other but only in the sense of physical juxtaposition. Personally, they are not as present or as close to each other as a young wife at home is present to her husband who may be on a trip at the other side of the world. The empirical fact of friendship is the Waterloo of science and technology. Such friendship is an absolute scandal to science, for while not empirically explainable, it is the most empirical of all experiences. But although empirical, it always points to transcendence, to a union with each other.

Belief and Immortality

We see the primacy of person again when we consider the nature of faith or belief. Marcel tells us "in order to believe that . . . we must first believe in." In short, before we can believe any fact, we must first believe in the person who has related the fact. For the Christian, belief must first be in Christ, then in Christianity, first in the person, only then in dogmas.

Marcel even applies his insight into person to the problem of immortality. Hope, which is not to be confused with wish, is a basic virtue of man. While we can wish for the impossible, we can never hope for it. Hope implies the possible; tied to faith it is a desire for the expected, but which as yet cannot be fully known. Hope, reaching out toward the future, reveals a transcendent element in man (his own future) and argues forcibly for conexistence of immortality.

Yet immortality has nothing to do with the indestructibility of the ego, as it has been so often misunderstood since Descartes' time. Rather it concerns the indestructibility of the "we relationship," for Marcel begins not with the "I am," but the "we are."

More concretely, the death of a loved one is not to be construed as an event, a happening in a world of happenings. The one who lives is not a "survivor" or bypasser of the one who died. The beloved who died *must continue to be* in some way as can be seen by an analysis of mourning or grief. So long as mourning for the other is not confused with hysteria (and a feeling sorry for oneself), such mourning argues to the continued but not fully known presence of the other.

But here again we must bear in mind the diverse meanings of *presence*, as applied to persons. Were the other not to continue to be in some way, mourning, this most genuine and bone-wrenching of all human emotions would betray itself ontologically as would the virtue of hope, for both relate to the other who has died.

The insight is similar to that of the Viennese psychiatrist, Viktor Frankl. He points out that the greatest argument for the existence of water is the fact that men get thirsty. The same applies to arguments for God, says Frankl. The need for God is psychological, yes. But one cannot stop there, as though an explanation has been reached, for the psychological itself needs a grounding in something deeper—some basis that reflects the ontological relationship between all of reality. Mourning for the other, then, implies a psychology of grief, but more than this, it implies a relationship to the other who has assumed a new mode of presence. In a certain sense, it is impossible by death to "lose" a friend, for one can lose only what one has or possesses and a friend is not in the category of *having*, but that of *being*.

Conclusion

Many think that Gabriel Marcel has brought philosophy back to its source, its home and original inspiration, the human person. Where it would fly off into the systematic and abstract, he has restored its reflective nature focusing at all times on the concrete. As he puts it so well, metaphysics should deal less with the problem of the "one and the many" than it should with the "full and the empty."

When Marcel was converted to Catholicism in 1929, many expected him to favor the philosophy of Thomism, always given a preferential place in the Church. However, Marcel regarded both Thomism and Marxism as dogmatisms rather than philosophies. For himself, he reserved the title "a philosopher of the threshold." For such a man as he describes it, "the stage always remains to be set; in a sense everything always starts from zero, and a philosopher is not worthy of the name unless he not only accepts but wills this harsh necessity." As a Catholic, he announced his openness to reality and revelation, although these are not necessarily to be construed as two different worlds.

Marcel has influenced many in the area of philosophy and religion. We see the latter especially becoming more person-oriented. Since he issues a call for the person to "know himself," he has gone full circle to that same command as Socrates. It is a command at once simple and complex. It is one that should not be ignored, least of all by philosophers who of all persons, should be true to themselves.

GABRIEL MARCEL

Review Questions

1. In what ways did Marcel's life affect his philosophical outlook?
2. Why is the view that reality is a spectacle akin to idealism?
3. Is technology and the emphasis on science in our age the cause of depersonalization? Explain.
4. Give an example of a functional relation in your own life.
5. Why is it incorrect and misleading to compare the brain to the computer, rather than the computer to the brain—or perhaps are both comparisons misleading?
6. What are the subtle but important differences between curiosity and wonder; individual and person; problem and mystery?
7. Elaborate on some various meanings *and* implications of "presence."
8. Man needs to have hope. Is this only a psychological need or is it an indication of something more basic? Explain.
9. What is Marcel's point in saying philosophy should rather speak of "the full and the empty" than the "one and the many?"
10. Describe the "breakthroughs" friendship makes with regard to a knowledge of oneself.

Special Thought Question

Is any natural being, besides man, able to reflect—to turn in on its thoughts about who or what it is? What are the implications for man's ability to do so?

BIBLIOGRAPHY

Primary Source: *Creative Fidelity.* Tr. Robert Rosthal (New York: Farrar, Strauss & Giroux, 1964). (Meditations on major Marcellian themes such as the person, faith, etc.)

CONCLUDING ESSAY

It is a truism to say that philosophy belongs to the ages. Like death and taxes, though, it will continue as long as man does. True to its symbol, the Owl of Minerva, philosophy takes off only after dark. That is why philosophy is not so much predictive (as are the sciences) but reflective. It "bakes no bread" we are told, yet as Walter Lippmann, the political philosopher mused:

> The role of philosophers is rarely, no doubt, creative. But it is critical, in that they had a deciding influence in determining what may be believed, how it can be believed, and what cannot be believed. The philosophers, one might say, stand at the very crossroads. While they may not cause the traffic to move, they can stop it and start it, they can direct it one way or the other. . . . In the familiar daylight world we cannot act as if ideas had no consequences. (*The Public Philosophy*)

Whether we consciously intend it or not, each of us formulates a basic outlook or philosophy of life. The overall result of this is to enable us clearly to determine what intrinsic meaning life and the world have for man. Even those who deny such meaning, as Nietzsche and Sartre, themselves espouse the cause of philosophy, for even an anti-metaphysics is still in the final analysis, its own kind of metaphysics or philosophy.

Just as philosophy judges, it too is subject to judgement. Yet this is not so much by disciplines external to itself, such as the various arts and sciences, as by its own inner demands. These inner demands, set forth as criteria for a philosophy that is meant to be fully meaningful and relevant, are basically seven in number. They are nicely enumerated and discussed by Virgilius Ferm in his simple and clear, *Basic Philosophy for Beginners*. We can do no better then list them directly. Philosophy must be:

1. Comprehensive—encompassing.
2. Harmonious—that is, in some way systematic.
3. Vital—having meaning for life.
4. Disciplined—built upon a hard logic of thought.
5. Consonant with reality—at one with the world in which we live.
6. Capable of revision—flexible with respect to a changing world.
7. Forged out of its own kind of thinking—truly real and truly philosophical.

Now that we have studied some representative thinkers in philosophy, it would be interesting to go back over them and apply the above criteria. Perhaps we would see that some philosophers—as well as countless others who have not been covered—have slipped through the cracks, as it were. They fall outside of the categories we want to impose on them and their philosophy. We need not be embarrassed by this, for philosophical ideas flow out of various media, whether of poetry, music, political science, economics, religion, etc. Reality is too large to be encompassed by any one individual and it certainly is too large to be confined to any single perspective of any one system of philosophy. We are reminded by Aristotle that truth is like the broad side of a barn. We can't miss it, yet to strike the bulls eye of the target painted on the barn, and to do so consistently, is difficult indeed. This is why one should hold no fears in trying to philosophize for oneself. One should entertain no false humility which prevents one from getting started in the quest for wisdom. It is never too soon to do it, nor is it ever too late to do so. In the final analysis philosophy is and continues to be the original do-it-yourself project. And it is a life long affair, both of the heart and of the head.

Simply knowing the ideas of other philosophers is not philosophy but the history of philosophy. While the importance of the history of philosophy must never be underestimated, that history is merely the laboratory within which one examines and scrutinizes ideas. But the acid test of ideas always will be the extent to which they square with experience and its interpretation. I might add, with one's own experience! That after all is where philosophy and its penetrating questions have their origin and that is where eventually they see their resolution in truth, value, and application.

Philosophy then is truly a "long row to hoe." So get going! And good luck!

SOME EXERCISES IN
THINKING AND REFLECTING

Regardless of the kind of philosophy to which one might subscribe, it will always involve *thinking* and *reflecting*. To be consistent, philosophical thinking needs practice such that it becomes habit forming. It involves analyzing a statement, problem or issue and trying to assess its meaning(s) and worth. In attempting this, one needs to uncover assumptions and make explicit the implications and consequences the issue entails. In short, a philosophical mind always is one that *thinks through* a problem — all the way through!

Reflecting on an issue implies considering the subject matter in a quiet and calm way, so as to determine its general meaning and especial meaning for you personally. Not that one must be "caught up" in every philosophical problem, however. Some issues just do not lend themselves to that. However, of the philosophers covered in this volume, virtually everyone has something to say to each of us. It is important to discover what that is and how it applies to one's own life situation.

To help train ourselves in the habit of thought which we call philosophical, then, there follows a number of insights, pithy sayings, *bon mots*, and controversial statements which are meant to provoke your attention so as to entice you to think about them. Do think about them, reflect upon them and discuss them with others. Try to provide reasons for your agreement or disagreement and try these out on others who have read them. See if you can apply them beyond their immediate context and give several concrete instances in which they are exemplified. All provide the philosopher with his daily fare—food for thought.

Permit me to illustrate an example of this exercise. Let us take the saying of Epictetus, a Greek philosopher slave freed by the Romans. He tells us that "If you would be virtuous, be virtuous!" "So what else is new?" you might respond. But it's not as simple as that. The statement implies a number of things. One is that a fundamental act of the will, of commitment is involved in being virtuous. And that takes discipline! Another is that virtue is a kind of habit, a good habit, which can be won only through constant practice. He is saying that there is nothing complicated about becoming virtuous; there is no need to learn various strategies and techniques. Just get started and do it. And do it today! In this, we see that the best advice is often the simplest.

Now, apply his principle to other activities, such as writing. How does one become a writer. It is not easy and most writers have to "sweat blood" for each word that pours forth. Many, such as students doing a term paper, will stall in various ways, e.g., look at the ceiling, resharpen a pencil, go to the store for more paper, (just in case they might run out of it), suggest to themselves that they might better postpone the writings until later, since they will have more free time, be relaxed, etc. The real thing to do if they would write, is to *start writing!* How simple, yet how difficult. We see here, as in the above example, the need for what the Germans call *Sitzfleisch*, loosely translated as discipline. The little statement by Epictetus then says it all. It is packed with meaning and implication.

A final example is that of a father of young children asking his good friend, "How can I stop hollering at my kids?" The friend's reply, "Stop hollering." Sound advice! Note that in all three examples cited, the implicit presence of the saying of the Greek oracle, "Know thyself."

It is time now to try your own hand at analyzing and reflecting. Materials for this are given below. As you go through them, look for similar statements in your various readings and make up your own list.

1. "The individual is the sole agent of the renewal of civilization." Albert Schweitzer.
2. "Philosophy is characterized by uncertainty. Indeed, its value is sought largely in its very uncertainty." Bertrand Russell.
3. "The uncultured mind is fascinated by the extraordinary; the cultured mind is fascinated by the ordinary." George Santyana.
4. "Gray is all theory; green is life's growing tree." Johanne Goethe.
5. "The intellectual vigor of a man, like that of a science, is measured by the dose of skepticism and doubt which he is capable of digesting and assimilating." Ortega y Gasset.
6. "Truth is a value and that is why we can live the truth and suffer and die for it." Gabriel Marcel.
7. "He was a good man—in the worse sense of the term." Mark Twain.
8. "The medium is the message and the massage." Marshall McLuan.
9. "A circle is less vicious, the bigger it is." Anon.
10. "If you know the why, you'll find the how." Viktor Frankl.

11. "Fear of error is itself an error and if analyzed in its depths reveals a fear of truth itself." George Hegel.

12. "The voice of intellect is a soft one, but it does not rest 'til it has gained a hearing. Finally, after a countless number of rebuffs, it succeeds." Sigmund Freud.

13. "With the birth of a child, it is not so much that a new intellect has come into the world, as it is the eruption of a new will." Gilbert K. Chesterton.

14. "If you can float, it makes no difference how deep is the water." Soren Kierkegaard.

15. "The fanatic is one who having forgotten his goals redoubles his efforts." George Santyana.

16. "The prophecies of what the courts will do in fact, and nothing more pretentious, are what I mean by law." Oliver Wendell Holmes.

17. "When one really comes to think that death is the end of everything, then there is nothing worse than being alive." Leo Tolstoy.

18. "Philosophy is not a body of doctrine but an activity." Ludwig Wittgenstein.

19. "The victory is not gained by the men at arms, who manage the pike and the sword; but by the trumpeteers, drummers, and musicians of the army." David Hume.

20. "It is not the consciousness of men that determines their existence, but on the contrary, their social existence determines their consciousness." Karl Marx.

21. "To philosophize is to seek, and this is to imply that there are things to see and to say . . . and because it seeks to see, philosophy passes for impiety." Maurice Merleau-Ponty.

22. "I swear, gentlemen, that to be too conscious is an illness, a real though-going disease." Feodor Dostoevsky.

23. "It is not tragic that we aren't masters of our fate: what would be tragic is if we were the total masters of our fate." Dom Aelrad Graham.

24. "The proof for God's existence lies in His inhumanity." Anton Chekov.

25. "For it was not so much by the knowledge of words that I came to the understanding of things, as by my experience of things, I was enabled to follow the meaning of words." Plutarch.

26. "Doctors try and talk the sick or those who believe themselves sick out of the fear of death. But these institutions function effectively only when things are going well with the individual. The life-order cannot dispel the dread which is part of every individual's life." Karl Jaspers.

27. "Young caterpillar to older caterpillar: "How can I believe there's a butterfly inside you or me when all I see is a fuzzy worm?" Trina Paulus.

28. "Subjectivity marks the frontier which separates the world of philosophy from that of religion." Jacques Maritain.
29. "The chief danger to philosophy is narrowness in the selection of evidence." Alfred North Whitehead.
30. "We live as we dream as we die—alone." Joseph Conrad.

GLOSSARY OF "ISMS"

Basic Explanations of Representative Philosophical Viewpoints

Agnosticism—We cannot transcend the material order to a knowledge of what, if anything, is beyond. Thus, we can neither confirm nor deny with certainty the existence of God, immortality of the soul, etc.

Deism—God exists and originally had something to do with the world, but now He is no longer concerned with it or with us in any way.

Determinism—Every event in the order of nature is wholly explained from without in terms of its invariable antecedent ("cause"). If applied to human nature, it rules out the possibility of free will. Similar to mechanism.

Dualism—All reality can be explained in terms of only two principles or two things. E.g., Descartes' use of matter and mind.

Dynamism—Reality is ultimately constituted of active points of force or energy.

Empiricism—Knowledge is exclusively a product of sense experience. Reason contributes nothing and cannot transcend sense experience.

Existentialism—A philosophical movement only loosely connected by emphasis given to man and the concrete meanings of human existence, freedom, anguish, paradox and absurdity, etc. Cf. Kierkegaard and Sartre.

Fideism—The only certain knowledge we can attain is that achieved by faith.

Hylemorphism—The Aristotelian explanation of corporeal substances in terms of an essential union of two principles, matter and form.

154

Hylozoism—The theory which holds that all reality is alive in some form or another.

Idealism—The view which affirms that the order of reality is the order of ideas. Hence, ideas are most real.

Innatism—Man's knowledge, in whole or in part, comes not from experience, but from preconceptions already found in the soul at birth, placed there by God or some other source.

Logical Positivism—Any philosophical conclusion that cannot be tested exclusively through sense experiences is valueless and meaningless.

Materialism—All reality is matter, generally in terms of quantity or extension.

Mechanism—Like art, a thing is entirely determined from without. We understand a thing if we understand its parts—the whole is no greater than the parts. The principle of inertia rules all, finality is denied in nature, and generally, quantity and local motion explain all reality.

Monism—One principle explains all reality. E.g., Those who claim all reality is material are monists.

Mysticism—Man can acquire a special super-knowledge beyond what reason or the senses convey to him. This may be achieved by some kind of communion or inspiration with the Divine or some fundamental cosmic principle. Such knowledge which is often moral and religious in nature is restrictive, individual and incommunicable.

Naturalism—Only nature is. There is no supernatural order. The world is self-existent and self-explanatory. Some form of evolutionism usually prevails which explains the higher coming from the lower.

Nominalism—The position which denies that the idea represents a nature grasped in a universal way. Ideas can only be of particular or individuals. Hence, the universal is just a *name*.

Occasionalism—The only genuine causality in the world is exercised by God; man, however, can provide the opportunity (occasion) for God to exercise that causality.

Panlogism—Usually the philosophy of Hegel which identified metaphysics with logic, and thereby explained all reality in terms of logical analysis and synthesis.

Pantheism—Everything is a part, a mode, or a manifestation of one supreme reality, God.

Pluralism—Reality is constituted by various distinct and separable principles.

Positivism—A form of empiricism. Only objects of sense experience can be known, hence, the impossibility of metaphysics in such a system. The only knowledge is that found in the positive sciences.

Pragmatism—An offshoot of utilitarianism. The true or good is the useful, hence, their relative character. Appeal is often made to will and faith rather than reason.

Rationalism—Reality can be explained solely in terms of intellectual analysis. The intellect can unfold (Hegel) or be creative (Kant) and supplies the principle of intelligibility to things. Knowledge is more from reason than from sense experience.

Realism—Recognition is given to the real or extra-mental world which is pluralistic and independent of a finite knower, but which can be known by him.

Scepticism—The view that man cannot attain truth or certitude about anything.

Scientism—The view that only natural science can supply us with worthwhile knowledge.

Stoicism—The moral view that we should be indifferent to the vicissitudes of the world.

Teleology—A doctrine upholding the reality of purpose in the universe. Every agent acts for an end. Opposed to mechanism.

Transcendental Idealism—(Critical Idealism). The philosophy of Kant. Although determination of knowledge is given by mind (forms or categories), the matter (phenomena) is given from without by experience. Hence, while essentially a species of idealism, it goes beyond (transcends) the ideal of admitting contact, in a limited way, with the extra-mental.